Nick Vandome

Android Phones
for Seniors

4th edition
Illustrated using Android 13

In easy steps is an imprint of In Easy Steps Limited
16 Hamilton Terrace · Holly Walk · Leamington Spa
Warwickshire · United Kingdom · CV32 4LY
www.ineasysteps.com

Fourth Edition

In Easy Steps Limited supports The Forest Stewardship Council (FSC),
the leading international forest certification organization. All our titles
that are printed on Greenpeace approved FSC certified paper carry the
FSC logo.

MIX
Paper from
responsible sources
FSC® C020837

Printed and bound in the United Kingdom

ISBN 978-1-78791-0140

Contents

1   **Introducing Android Phones**   7

About Android   8
About Android Phones   9
Updating Android   10
Android Overlays   11
Makes and Models   12
Features of Android 13   14
Features of Android Phones   16
SIM Cards   18
Setting Up Your Phone   19
Android and Google   20
Creating a Google Account   22
Using a Touchscreen   24
Using Apps   26

2   **Android Settings**   27

Accessing Settings   28
Communication Settings   29
Customization Settings   30
Security Settings   32
Organization Settings   34
Wellbeing and Accessibility Settings   36
Google and Phone Settings   38
Quick Settings   40

3   **Around an Android Phone**   41

Viewing the Home Screen   42
Navigating Around   43
Adding Apps to Home   46
Moving Apps   47

Working with Favorites   48
Creating Folders   49
Adding Widgets   50
Changing the Background   52
Using Notifications   54
Locking Your Phone   56
Searching   58
Google Assistant Search   60
Hey Google   62
Using Google Discover   65

4 Calls and Contacts   67

Adding Contacts   68
Saving Contacts from Calls   70
Saving Contacts from Texts   71
Editing Contacts   72
Managing Contacts   74
Making a Call   76
Receiving a Call   78
Setting Ringtones   81

5 Using the Keyboard   83

Keyboards with Android   84
Selecting Keyboards   85
About the Google Keyboard   86
Keyboard Settings   88
Gboard Suggestion Strip   90
General Keyboard Shortcuts   92
Adding Text   93
Working with Text   94

6 Messaging and Email 95

Texting Contacts	96
Using Emojis	98
Adding Attachments	100
Sending a Voice Note	101
Setting Up Email	102
Using Gmail	104
Going Hands-free	106

7 Android Apps 107

Apps for Android	108
Google Apps	110
Maps	112
Notes and Memos	114
Social Media	115
Health and Fitness	116
Playing Games	117
Around the Play Store	118
Finding Apps	120
Downloading Apps	122
Uninstalling Apps	124
Updating Apps	126
App Information	128

8 Being Entertained 129

Music on Android	130
Media Player	134
Google TV	135
Obtaining Ebooks	138
Around an Ebook	140

9 Getting Things Done 141

Google Productivity Apps 142
Google Drive 143
Google Docs 146
Google Sheets 150
Google Slides 152

10 Keeping in the Picture 153

Using Cameras 154
Adding Photos 156
Viewing Photos 158
Adding Albums 161
Editing Photos 162
Sharing Photos 164

11 Online with Chrome 165

Android Web Browsers 166
Opening Pages 167
Bookmarking Pages 168
Links and Images 170
Using Tabs 171
Being Incognito 172
Browser Settings 173

12 Staying Secure 175

Security Issues 176
About Antivirus Apps 177
Security and Privacy 178
Digital Wellbeing 182
Parental Controls 184
Locating Your Phone 186

Index 187

1 Introducing Android Phones

Smartphones using the Android operating system are the most used phones worldwide. This chapter gives an overview of Android on a smartphone, to get started using it. It also looks at creating a Google Account for using Google services on your Android phone.

8   About Android

9   About Android Phones

10 Updating Android

11 Android Overlays

12 Makes and Models

14 Features of Android 13

16 Features of Android Phones

18 SIM Cards

19 Setting Up Your Phone

20 Android and Google

22 Creating a Google Account

24 Using a Touchscreen

26 Using Apps

Android is based on the flexible and robust Linux operating system and shares many similarities with it.

Android on a Google Pixel is the purest form of the operating system since, unlike other manufacturers who use Android on their phones, there is no customization to the operating system. The examples in this book are provided using a Google Pixel with Android 13, the most widely used version of Android at the time of printing.

The **New** icon pictured above indicates a new or enhanced feature introduced with Android phones using Android 13.

About Android

Android is essentially a mobile computing operating system – i.e. one for mobile devices such as smartphones and tablets.

Android is an open source operating system, which means that the source code is made available to hardware manufacturers and developers so that they can design their devices and apps in conjunction with Android. This has created a large community of Android developers, and also means that Android is not tied to one specific device; individual manufacturers can use it (as long as they meet certain specific criteria), which has led to Android being available on a variety of different devices.

Android Inc. was founded in 2003, and the eponymous operating system was initially developed for mobile devices. Google quickly saw this as an opportunity to enter the smartphone and tablet market and bought Android in 2005. The first Android-powered smartphone appeared in 2008 and since then has gone from strength to strength. Android-based smartphones have a majority of the worldwide market, and Android is used by numerous manufacturers on their handsets.

The main differences between the Android mobile operating system and desktop- or laptop-based ones such as Windows or macOS are:

- **No file structure**. There is no default built-in file manager structure for storing and managing files. All content is saved within the app in which it is created.

- **Self-contained apps**. Because there is no file structure, apps are generally self-contained and do not communicate with each other, unless required.

- **Numerous Home screens**. There are numerous Home screens on an Android phone, and they can be used to store and access apps.

- **Generally, content is saved automatically as it is created**. Apps save content as it is created, so there is no Save or Save As function within many apps.

About Android Phones

Android has been used on smartphones since 2008. Initially adoption was fairly slow, but this has now accelerated to the point where Android is the most widely used operating system on smartphones.

Combinations of Android phones

Since Android can be used by different manufacturers, this means that a range of the latest smartphones always run on Android. In addition, since not all older phones are designed to be upgraded to the latest version of Android, there are phones running several different versions of Android – for instance, the Google Pixel 6 runs the latest version of Android (at the time of printing, Android 15), while some models of older phones may still only be able to run Android 10 or earlier. As a result, there are hundreds of combinations in terms of smartphone models and versions of Android on the market. Some are the expensive flagship models, which will run a relatively new version of Android (although not necessarily the very latest version) compared with cheaper models that can only run an older version of Android.

Checking for versions of Android

When buying an Android phone, look at the version of Android in the phone's specification. Ideally, it should be a relatively new version in order to enable it to be upgraded to the latest version when it becomes available. Some models of Android phones reach a point where they do not have the required hardware to update to the next version of Android and are therefore stuck with the current version that they are using. This may also limit the phone's ability to download and use the latest apps that are available.

Android phone differences

Despite the variations in versions of Android, the user experience is generally similar on different Android phones. However, one area of difference is in the hardware used by manufacturers. For instance, some newer Android phones have face recognition (**Face Unlock**) or fingerprint sensors for unlocking the phone, and others have more sophisticated cameras.

Updated versions of Android were historically named alphabetically after items of confectionery but are now named numerically.

Due to the range of versions of Android on smartphones, it is not feasible to cover all possibilities across different manufacturers. Therefore, this book will focus on the standard functionality of Android that is available through all versions of the operating system.

Updating Android

Since Android is open source and can be used on a variety of different devices, this can sometimes cause delays in updating the operating system on the full range of eligible Android devices. This is because it has to be tailored specifically for each different device; it is not a case of "one size fits all." This can lead to delays in the latest version being rolled out to all compatible devices. The product cycle for new versions is usually six to nine months.

As Android is a Google product, Google's own devices are usually the first ones to run the latest version of the software. Therefore, the Google Pixel was the first phone to run the latest version of Android – 15 – while others are still running previous versions, covering a range of releases over several years. The majority of Android phones have versions that are usually at least a couple of years behind the latest version, with Android 13 currently being the most widely used. For recently released phones, an upgrade to the latest version of Android will be scheduled into the update calendar or it might be already available to install. However, for some older Android phones the latest version of the software is not always made available, usually because of hardware limitations within the phones.

Much of the general functionality of the Android operating system is the same, regardless of the version being used.

For more details about Android settings, see Chapter 2.

The version of the Android operating system that is being used on your phone can be viewed from within the **System update** section of the **Settings** app. This is where details of the current version of Android can be viewed.

Settings

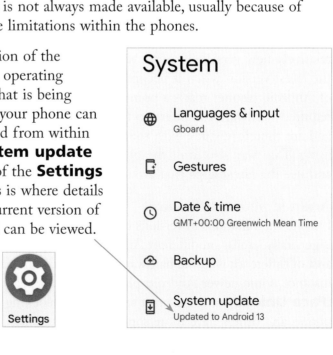

System

🌐 **Languages & input**
Gboard

📱 **Gestures**

🕐 **Date & time**
GMT+00:00 Greenwich Mean Time

☁ **Backup**

📲 **System update**
Updated to Android 13

Android Overlays

Because Android is an open source operating system, it means that manufacturers can amend it, to a certain extent, when they add it to their phone models. This keeps the core Android operating system, but the user interface can be adapted so that it becomes specific to each manufacturer. This is known as an "overlay" and means that the appearance of Android will be different on, for instance, a Samsung phone and an HTC one. However, the operation of Android will still be the same on different brands of phones and, in most cases, the appearance of the user interface will be very similar and still recognizable as Android.

If you are familiar with one brand of Android phone and then switch to another, it may take a little while to get used to the overlay of the new phone. However, the underlying functionality should be the same.

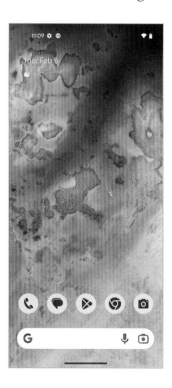

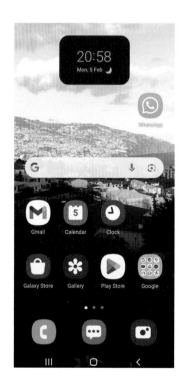

In addition to overlays, manufacturers can also add their own apps to their brand of Android phone and, in some cases, have their own app store for downloading more apps.

The one phone that does not have any kind of overlay is the Google Pixel: since Google owns Android, it uses the operating system in its purest form on its phones.

Beware

Check the overall size of any phone in which you are interested to ensure it fits in one hand comfortably. Also, check the weight to make sure that it is not too heavy.

Don't forget

"Selfies" are photos taken of yourself, using the front-facing camera (on the screen of the phone).

Makes and Models

There is a significant range of companies that manufacture Android smartphones, and some of the features to look for in any of them are:

- Display screen size, which is measured diagonally.

- RAM (random-access memory). This is the internal memory that processes the operation of the phone. Look for a minimum of 4-6 gigabytes (GB).

- Memory. This is the internal memory for storing content. Look for a minimum of 64-128 GB.

- Operating system. Look for the version of Android being used and the latest version to which it is upgradable.

- Main camera. This is used for most photo options (except selfies), and the larger the megapixels (MP) count, the better. Look for a minimum of 48 MP.

- Face ID or fingerprint sensor for unlocking the phone.

- Battery. Look for a battery with as long a charge life as possible, and also fast-charging capabilities.

Samsung

Samsung is the market leader in terms of the number of smartphones sold globally, partly due to the fact that it offers a considerable range of models, including its flagship Galaxy range. Several Samsung smartphones models use the TouchWiz interface as an overlay for Android.

Google Pixel

Since Android is owned by Google, it makes sense for it to have its own Android phone, the Google Pixel, which comes in a standard model or in a Pro model. The Google Pixel is a high-specification smartphone and, unlike the majority of Android phones on the market, comes with the latest version of Android (15 at the time of printing). Also, the Google Pixel will be the first phone that can update to the next version of Android when it is released.

Sony

Sony is another major player in the smartphone market and has a reputation for producing phones with particularly high-quality cameras. The flagship Sony Android phone is the Xperia range.

Huawei

Huawei is a major Chinese technology company that produces a wide range of communications devices, including smartphones. Most Huawei phones that use Android also use the Emotion User Interface (EMUI) overlay.

HTC

HTC is a Taiwanese company that was at the forefront of the development of smartphones using the Android operating system. Despite an up-and-down performance in the smartphone market, HTC has produced a successful range of phones, with one of the high-end models being the HTC Desire Pro.

Nokia

Nokia has a long history of producing cell/mobile phones, and although there have been some breaks for the Nokia brand, it is again well established, with a range of smartphones that run on Android.

Lenovo

Lenovo is a large Chinese technology company that produces personal computers, laptops, tablets and smartphones. It owns the Motorola brand, which has its own website, and now uses this branding for its smartphones instead of using the Lenovo brand.

Motorola

Although the Motorola brand is owned by Lenovo and sold via its website with this branding, Motorola smartphones can also be bought from the Motorola website, with particular emphasis on the **moto g** range.

Different geographical regions can offer their own ranges of Android smartphones.

13

Features of Android 13

Although Android 14 and 15 are both newer versions than Android 13, they are only available on a limited number of Android phones, and version 13 has a higher adoption rate. The majority of features are the same as for earlier versions of Android and are consistent across different brands of Android phone. However, there are also some new Android 13 features:

The features on these two pages are all updates from previous versions of Android.

Customizable app icons

Android 13 offers a customization option so that the app icons on your Home screen can be changed to have the same overall color theme as the background being used. If the background changes, then so does the color theme for the app icons. This customization feature can be applied in the **Wallpaper & style** category of the **Settings** app, using the **Themed icons** option.

Notifications

The way in which notifications are dealt with is another feature that has been updated in Android 13. **In Settings > Notifications** there is a range of options for managing notifications, and when a new app is opened, the default option that appears enables you to immediately allow, or not allow, notifications to be sent from this app. This means that you can always be in control of which notifications appear.

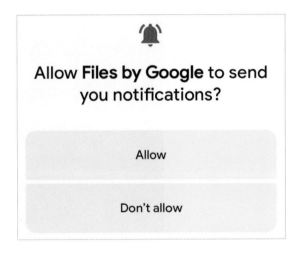

Updated Media Player

The Media Player that is provided with Android 13, for playing music and podcasts, has also been updated. This includes displaying cover artwork when an item is playing, and also an animated playback bar at the bottom of the Media Player that oscillates when an item is playing. The new Media Player does not work with all apps, particularly some non-Google ones.

Beware

The new Media Player is only activated when the Lock screen is on and music or podcasts are already playing. If the phone is unlocked, the content will play in its own app.

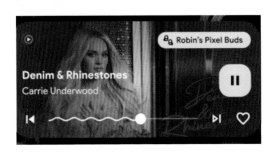

Features of Android Phones

The button for turning a phone on and off is located on the side of the body of the device in most cases, as are the other buttons and ports that can be used for various functions on your phone.

On/Off button

This can also be used to put the phone into **Sleep** mode. Press and hold for a couple of seconds to turn on the phone. Press once to put it to sleep or wake it up from sleep.

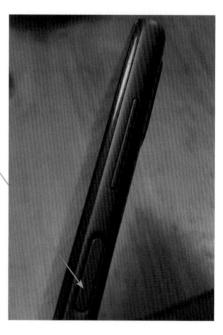

Don't forget

If the Android operating system is updated on a phone, it will probably restart before the update takes effect.

Turning off

To turn off an Android phone, press and hold on the **On/Off** button until the **Power off** button appears on the screen. Tap on this to turn the phone off. Tap on **Restart** to shut down the phone and then start it again.

Emergency   Power off

Restart

Volume button

This is either a single button on the opposite side to the **On/Off** button or two separate buttons. Press the buttons to adjust the volume.

Cameras

There is the main, rear-facing camera (on the back of the phone) for taking pictures. Most phones also have a front-facing camera (on the screen side of the phone), which is usually a lower resolution and is useful for making video calls or taking "selfies" (see page 12), as the user can view the screen at the same time as using the camera.

Headphone jack

This is used to connect a headphone cable and is usually at the top or bottom of the phone.

Micro USB port

This can be used to attach the phone to an adapter for charging the phone or to a computer for charging or to download content from (or upload to) the phone, using the supplied USB cable. Once the phone is connected to a computer it will show up as a removable drive in the file manager, in the same way as an item such as a flashdrive.

microSD cards

These can be inserted into the appropriate slot on the body of the phone to increase the amount of storage for items such as photos and music.

Hot tip

An increasing number of phones, particularly the higher-end models, have a fingerprint sensor on the body of the phone that can be used to unlock the phone with a unique fingerprint. Fingerprint sensors have to be set up by using the applicable item (usually in the **Settings** app) and then pressing on the sensor several times so that it can identify your unique fingerprint. More than one fingerprint can usually be set up for use with the sensor (see pages 56-57 for details about how to set this up). Some phones also use face recognition for unlocking the phone.

SIM Cards

The SIM card for your Android phone will be provided by your mobile carrier – i.e. the company that provides your cellular phone and data services. Without this, you would still be able to communicate using your phone, but only via Wi-Fi and compatible services. A SIM card gives you access to a mobile network too. Android phones have a slot on the side (a SIM tray) for inserting a SIM card. To insert a SIM card into the SIM tray:

Don't forget

SIM cards usually use 3G, 4G or 5G networks for providing cellular phone and data services – e.g. texting and messaging. 5G is the fastest, but is not currently as widely available as 4G. The G in the name stands for Generation.

Don't forget

Some models of Android phones also have an option to use an eSIM. An eSIM is a digital SIM that allows you to activate a mobile data plan from your network provider without having to use a physical SIM card. eSIM cards can be more secure as there are no physical cards to be removed.

1 The SIM tray is located on the side of the phone, with a small hole at the end of it

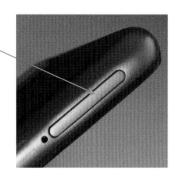

2 Use the SIM tool (which should be provided with the phone) to open the SIM tray, by pressing firmly into the hole shown in Step 1

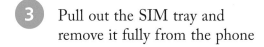

3 Pull out the SIM tray and remove it fully from the phone

4 Insert the SIM card into the SIM tray and return it into the slot in the phone. (Some SIM trays have compartments for different sizes of SIM cards)

Setting Up Your Phone

When you first turn on your phone (by pressing and holding the **On/Off** button), you will be taken through the setup process. This only has to be done once, and some of the steps can be completed or amended at a later time, usually within the **Settings** app. Some of the elements that can be applied during the setup process include:

- **Language**. This option lets you select the language to use for your phone. Whichever language is selected will affect all of the system text on the phone, and it will also apply to all user accounts on the phone.

- **Wi-Fi**. This can be used to set up your Wi-Fi so that you can access web and online services. In the **Select Wi-Fi** window, tap on the name of your router. Enter the password for your router and tap on the **Connect** button.

- **Google Account**. At this stage, you can create a Google Account or sign in with an existing one. Once you have done this, you will have full access to Google Account services and you will not have to enter your login details again. (A Google Account can also be set up at a later time; see pages 22-23.)

- **Google services**. This includes options for which of the Google services you want to use, including backing up your phone, using location services, and sending feedback to Google.

- **Date and time**. This can be used to set the date and time, either manually or automatically.

- **Method of screen lock**. This can be used to set a lock for the phone, using a fingerprint, a PIN code, a pattern, a password, or face recognition.

- **Screen layout**. This can be used to create a larger interface on the phone's screen, by changing the size of items on it and the font size.

Most routers require a password when they are accessed for the first time by a new device. This is a security measure to ensure that other people cannot gain unauthorized access to your router and Wi-Fi.

Wi-Fi has to be connected in order for a Google Account to be created or signed in to during the setting up of the phone.

Since Android is owned by Google, much of its functionality is provided through a Google Account.

Don't forget

If you already have a Gmail Account, this will also serve as your Google Account, and the login details (email address and password) can be used for both.

Don't forget

When you buy anything through your Google Account, such as music, apps or movies, you will have to enter your credit or debit card details (unless you are downloading a free app), which will be used for future purchases through your Google Account.

Android and Google

Most phones are linked to specific companies for the provision of their services and selection of apps: Apple for the iPhone and Google for phones using Android, as well as the phone's manufacturer (e.g. Samsung). As with other phones, for Android phones you must have a linked account to get the most out of your phone. This is a Google Account and is created free of charge with a Google email address (Gmail) and a password. Once it has been created, your Google Account will give you access to a number of pre-installed Android apps and also additional services such as backing up and storing your content online.

When you first set up your phone, you can enter your Google Account details or select to create a new account. You can also do this at any time by accessing one of the apps that requires access to a Google Account. These include:

- **Play Store**, for obtaining more apps.

- **Google TV**, for obtaining movies and TV shows.

- **Play Books**, for obtaining books.

- **Google News**, for displaying news stories.

When you access one of these apps you will be prompted to create a Google Account. You do not have to do so at this point, but it will give you access to the full range of Google Account services.

Other apps such as the **Photos** app for storing and viewing photos can be used on their own, but if a Google Account has been set up, the content can be backed up automatically.

G

Sign in

with your Google Account.
Learn more about using your account

Email or phone

Forgot email?

Create account

Next

...cont'd

Some of the benefits of a Google Account include:

- Access from any computer or mobile device with web access, from the **accounts.google.com/** page. Once you have entered your account details you can access online Google services, including Calendar, Gmail, and the Play Store.

- Keep your content synchronized and backed up. With a Google Account, all of your linked data will be automatically synchronized so that it is available for all web-enabled devices, and it will also be backed up by Google's own computers (servers). Some items can also be backed up manually rather than automatically.

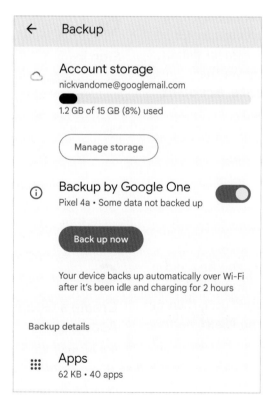

If you buy items from the Play Store through your Google Account on the web, they will also be available on your Android phone.

A new Google Account can also be created within **Settings > Passwords & accounts** on your phone. Tap on the **Add account** button and tap on the **Google** button. Then, enter the required details for the new Google Account (see pages 22-23).

- Peace of mind that your content is protected. There is a **Security** section on your Google Account web page where you can apply various security settings and alerts.

21

Creating a Google Account

A new Google Account can be created in the following different ways:

● During the initial setup of your Android phone.

● When you first access one of the relevant apps, as explained on page 20.

● From the **Settings** app, by selecting **Passwords & accounts** > **Add account**.

For each of the above, the process for creating a Google Account is the same.

Don't forget

During the account setup process there is also a screen for account recovery, where you can add an answer to a question so that your account details can be retrieved by Google if you forget them.

1 If you already have an account, enter your sign-in details, or tap on the **Create account** option

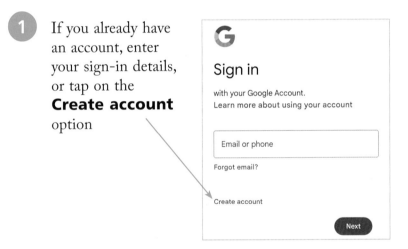

G

Sign in

with your Google Account.
Learn more about using your account

Email or phone

Forgot email?

Create account

Next

2 Enter the first and last name for the new account user, then tap on the **Next** button

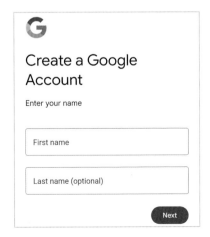

G

Create a Google Account

Enter your name

First name

Last name (optional)

Next

3 Enter a username (this will also become your Gmail address), then tap on the **Next** button at the bottom of the screen

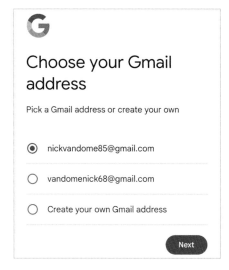

A username for a Google Account is a unique name created by the user, which is suffixed by *@gmail.com*.

4 Create a password for the account and then re-enter it for confirmation. Tap on the **Next** button at the bottom of the screen

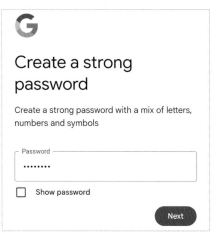

If your chosen username has already been taken, you will be prompted to amend it. This can usually be done by adding a sequence of numbers to the end of it, but make sure you remember the sequence correctly.

5 The account details are displayed. Tap on the **Next** button to sign in with your new account

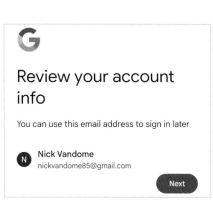

Using a Touchscreen

The traditional method of interacting with a computer is by using a mouse and a keyboard as the input devices. However, this all changed with smartphones; they are much more tactile devices that are controlled by tapping and swiping on the touchscreen. This activates and controls the apps and settings on the phone, and enables you to add content with the virtual keyboard that appears at appropriate times.

Gently does it

Touchscreens are sensitive devices and only require a light touch to activate the required command. To get the best out of your touchscreen:

Hot tip

If you are using your phone in an area where there is likely to be moisture, such as in the kitchen if you are following a recipe, cover the touchscreen in some form of light plastic wrap to protect it from any spills or splashes.

- Tap, swipe or press gently on the screen. Do not use excessive force and do not keep tapping with increasing pressure if something does not work in the way in which you expected. Instead, try performing another action and then returning to the original one.

- Tap with your fingertip rather than your fingernail. This will be more effective in terms of performing the required operation and is better for the surface of the touchscreen.

- For the majority of touchscreen tasks, tap, press or swipe at one point on the screen. The exception to this is zooming in and out on certain items (such as web pages), which can be done by swiping outward and pinching inward with thumb and forefinger.

- Keep your touchscreen dry, and make sure that your fingers are also clean and free of moisture.

- Use a cover to protect the screen when not in use, particularly if you are carrying your phone in a jacket pocket or a bag.

- Use a screen cloth to keep the screen clean and free of fingerprints and smears. The touchscreen should still work if it has fingerprints and marks on it, but it will become harder to see clearly what is on the screen.

Touchscreen controls

Touchscreens can be controlled with three main types of actions. These are:

- **Tapping**. Tap once on an item such as an app to activate it. This can also be used for the main navigation control buttons at the bottom of the touchscreen or for items such as **On/Off** buttons when applying settings for specific items.

For more information about working with apps on the Home screen and the Notifications panel, see Chapter 3.

- **Pressing**. Press and hold on an item on the Home screen to move its position or place it in the **Favorites Tray** at the bottom of the screen.

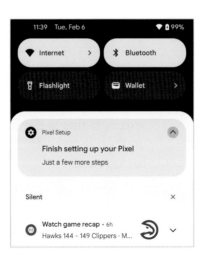

- **Swiping**. Swipe down from the top of the Home screen to access the **Notifications panel** and the **Quick Settings**, and swipe left and right to view all available Home screens or to scroll through photo albums.

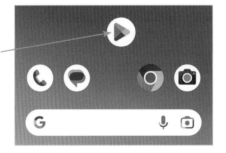

Using Apps

One of the great selling points for Android phones is the range of apps that are available for them. At the time of printing, there are at least 3.4 million Android apps in the Google Play Store, with others available from third-party developers. Some are free, while others are paid for.

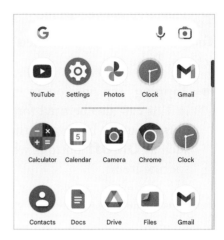

Don't forget

If your phone is running low on memory it will automatically close any open apps to free up more memory. The ones that have been inactive for the longest period of time are closed first.

The pre-installed apps are the ones that give the initial functionality to your phone, and include items such as email, a web browser, a calendar a calculator and maps. They appear as icons on your phone's Home screen or in the **All Apps** area (see page 46) and are accessed by tapping on them once.

Managing apps

When you switch from one app to another, you do not have to close down the original one that you were using. Android keeps it running in the background, but in a state of hibernation so that it is not using up any memory or processing power on your phone. To do this:

Don't forget

New apps for Android phones are available through the Play Store or directly from the developer's website. They can be downloaded from there and will then appear on your phone. (See pages 122-123.)

Play Store

1 Tap on an app to open it and move through its screens as required. Swipe up from the bottom of the screen to return to the Home screen (or tap on the **Home** button on the phone's Navigation bar at the bottom of the screen, if this is the method of navigation being used – see page 45). The app will remain open in the background

2 Tap on the app again. It will open up at the point at which you left it

2 Android Settings

Android phones have a range of settings that can be applied to specify the operation of the device, use security features, and customize its look and feel.

28 Accessing Settings

29 Communication Settings

30 Customization Settings

32 Security Settings

34 Organization Settings

36 Wellbeing and Accessibility Settings

38 Google and Phone Settings

40 Quick Settings

The settings have been updated with Android 13.

The **Settings** app can be added to the Home screen, or the Favorites Tray (see page 48), by pressing and holding on it in the **All Apps** section and then dragging it to the required location.

When using settings, tap on the left-facing arrowhead to return to the previous page within a specific setting or to return to the main **Settings** Homepage.

← **Do Not Disturb**

Accessing Settings

We all like to think of ourselves as individuals, and this extends to the appearance and operation of our electronic gadgets. An Android phone offers a range of settings so that you can set it up exactly the way you want, and give it your own look and feel. These are available from the **Settings** app.

To access the **Settings** app on your Android phone:

1 Swipe up from the bottom of the screen to access the **All Apps** section

2 Tap on the **Settings** app

Settings

3 The full range of settings is displayed

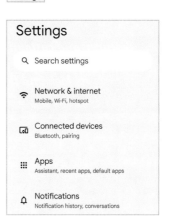

Settings

🔍 Search settings

📶 Network & internet
Mobile, Wi-Fi, hotspot

📱 Connected devices
Bluetooth, pairing

▦ Apps
Assistant, recent apps, default apps

🔔 Notifications
Notification history, conversations

4 Tap on an item to view all of the options for it. (If necessary, tap on the options at the next level down to see their own options)

←
Sound & vibration

Media volume

Call volume

Ring & notification volume

Alarm volume

Do Not Disturb
Off

Communication Settings

Some Android phones have different versions of the standard Android settings, but in general they are consistent across different devices – they can usually be grouped into general categories, such as communication, customization, security, organization, wellbeing and accessibility, and Google and phone. There are then specific settings options within these main categories.

Network & internet
These settings can include:

- **Internet/Wi-Fi**. This can be used to connect to a Wi-Fi router so that you can access the internet.

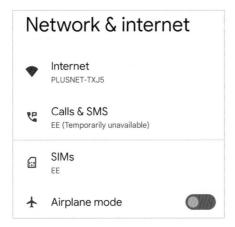

The **Wi-Fi** setting can be used to connect to Wi-Fi in your own home and also to any public Wi-Fi hotspots. For both, you will usually need to use a password to access the router.

- **Calls and SIM cards**. This displays details of the provider of your cell phone (mobile phone) service, including your phone's number and information about the SIM card in the phone.

- **Airplane mode**. This can be used to disable communication functions when on a flight.

Connected devices
These settings can be used to connect to other devices, usually using Bluetooth. There is usually a "pairing" option so that your phone and the device that you want to connect to can recognize each other and then share data and content.

Customization Settings

This group of settings can be used to customize your Android phone just the way you want it.

Sound & vibration

These settings can include:

- **Volume options**. These can be used to set the volume on your phone for a range of functions, from the volume for media playing on your phone to the volume of ringtones and alarms.

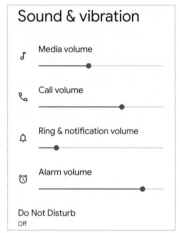

Sound & vibration

♪ Media volume

📞 Call volume

🔔 Ring & notification volume

⏰ Alarm volume

Do Not Disturb
Off

- **Do Not Disturb**. This can be used to specify times for when you do not want to be disturbed by calls or notifications. Exceptions can be added for specific people.

- **Vibrations and haptics**. This can be used to select options for vibrations and haptics, for how buttons respond when they are tapped or pressed.

- **Default sounds**. This can be used to select default sounds for items, including notifications and alarms.

- **Sounds**. This can be used to enable or disable sounds for a variety of tasks on the phone, including dial pad tones when making a phone call, screen

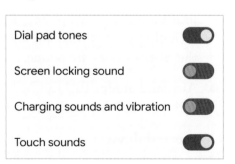

Dial pad tones

Screen locking sound

Charging sounds and vibration

Touch sounds

locking sounds, charging sounds and vibration for when the phone is fully charged, and touch sounds for using the keypad.

Display

These settings can include:

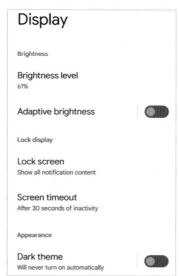

- **Brightness level**. This can be used to change the screen brightness.

- **Adaptive brightness**. This can be used to set the screen brightness automatically, based on the ambient lighting.

- **Lock screen**. This can be used to specify content that can appear on the Lock screen.

- **Screen timeout**. This can be used to specify a length of inactivity for the phone until the Lock screen is activated.

- **Dark theme**. This can be used to activate a dark theme when the phone recognizes that it is nighttime, which is done using the phone's clock.

- **Screen saver**. This can be used to activate a screen saver image when the phone is locked.

- **Night Light**. This can be used to limit the use of blue light on the phone at nighttime, to aid relaxation.

- **Display size and text**. This can be used to change the size of icons on the Home screen and also the text size displayed on the phone.

Wallpaper & style

These settings can be used to change the background wallpaper for the Lock screen and the Home screen. See Chapter 3, pages 52-53 for details.

Hot tip

The **Night Light** setting is an excellent option for relaxing in the evening. Another way to aid a good night's sleep is to turn your phone off completely at night.

Security Settings

This group of settings can be used to help make using your Android phone as safe and as secure as possible, for ultimate peace of mind.

Security & privacy

These settings can include:

- **App security**.

- **Device lock**.

- **Security Checkup**.

- **Find My Device**.

- **System updates**.

- **Privacy**.

Location

These settings can include:

For more information about the **Security & privacy** settings, see Chapter 12, pages 178-181.

- **App location permissions**. This can be used to allow apps to access your location. This can be done for all of the apps on your phone, or individual apps can be given this permission.

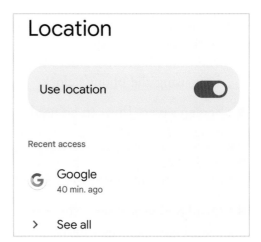

- **Location**. This can be used to enable location services for a range of items, not just apps on your phone accessing your location. This can include location services for being notified about local emergencies, such as earthquakes.

Safety & emergency

These settings can include:

- **Medical information**. This can be used to store your own important medical information that could be used in an emergency. This information can be set to be displayed on the Lock screen in an emergency.

- **Emergency contacts**. This can be used to add people for someone to contact if you suffer an emergency.

Safety & emergency

⬡ Open Personal Safety

🪪 Medical information
Name, blood type and more

👥 Emergency contacts
No information

SOS Emergency SOS
Managed by Personal Safety

🚗 Car crash detection
Sign in to Personal Safety

⏻ Crisis alerts
Sign in to Personal Safety

- **Emergency SOS**. This can be used to set up an option whereby your phone will call the emergency services automatically if you press the **On/Off** button an allocated number of times.

- **Car crash detection**. This can be used to detect whether you have been in a car crash and determine the appropriate action to take.

- **Crisis alerts**. This can be used to receive notifications if there are any natural disasters near to your location.

Passwords & accounts

These settings can include:

- **Passwords**. This can be used to view saved passwords that have been used on websites.

- **Autofill**. This can be used to enable passwords to be filled in automatically on websites.

- **Accounts**. This can be used to add accounts to your Android device, such as adding a new email account or a social media account.

Beware

Be careful when using **Autofill**, particularly if other people are going to be using your phone. This is because they could automatically log in to websites that require a password and access sensitive information.

Organization Settings

This group of settings can be used to view information about battery usage on your phone, its storage capacity, and also how notifications operate.

Battery

These settings can include:

The **Battery Saver** setting works by disabling a number of automatic tasks on your phone, such as automatically downloading new emails, so you will have to do these tasks manually.

Turning the **Battery percentage** setting **On** is a good option, as you can always see the exact amount of battery power that you have left in the status bar.

- **Battery usage**. This can be used to view the overall daily battery usage on your phone and also which apps have been using the most battery power.

Battery

82%

More than 2 days left

Battery usage
View usage since last full charge

Battery Saver
Off

- **Battery Saver**. This can be used to put your phone into a low power state, to save battery power if your phone's battery is running low.

- **Adaptive preferences**. This can be used to enable your phone to automatically use the battery most effectively when using apps and charging the battery.

- **Battery percentage**. This can be used to show the battery power percentage in the status bar at the top of the screen.

- **Battery widget**. This can be used to add the battery widget to the Home screen.

Notifications

These settings can be used to specify how notifications operate; see Chapter 3, pages 54-55 for details.

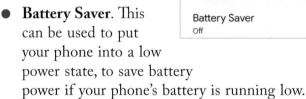

Notifications

Manage

App settings
Control notifications from individual apps

Notification history
Show recent and snoozed notifications

Storage

These settings can include showing how much storage capacity has been used on the phone's internal memory, which elements are using the most storage, and an option for freeing up space.

- **Free up space**. This can be used to remove items that are not being used by the phone, to free up more space. Any items that are removed can usually be reinstalled, if required.

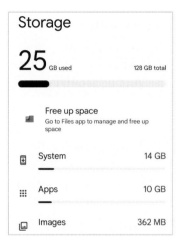

- **System**. This shows how much space the phone's system files are taking up – i.e. the operating system and files that are required for the phone to operate.

- **Apps**. This shows how much space is being used by apps on the phone, including pre-installed ones and any that have been downloaded from the Play Store.

- **Images**. This shows how much space is being used by photos and videos on the phone.

- **Games**. This shows how much space is being used by any games on the phone.

- **Trash**. This shows how much space is being used by items that have been deleted and moved to the Trash.

- **Audio**. This shows how much space is being used by audio files, such as voice memos recorded on the **Recorder** app.

- **Documents & other**. This shows how much space is being used by documents, such as word processing documents or spreadsheets.

Images and videos generally use up the most space on digital devices, so it is a good idea to regularly delete any items that you do not need.

To empty items out of the Trash permanently, tap on the **Trash** option, select the items to be removed, and then tap on the **Delete** button.

Wellbeing and Accessibility Settings

Digital Wellbeing & parental controls

These settings can include options for monitoring screen usage and also for adding restrictions if children or teens are using the phone. See Chapter 12, pages 182-185 for more details about these settings.

Accessibility

These settings cover a range of options for anyone who has accessibility issues in relation to using an Android phone. The **Accessibility** settings are usually included within the main category headings, which are:

The **Screen reader** option (**TalkBack**) has its own settings that can be applied to determine how the feature operates.

36

- **Screen reader**. This can be used to read what is on the screen, for users with visual impairment.

- **Display**. These settings can be used to change a range of options on the screen, such as text size and color.

- **Interaction controls**. This category provides a range of options for controlling your phone, rather than the usual navigation methods, for users with motor issues.

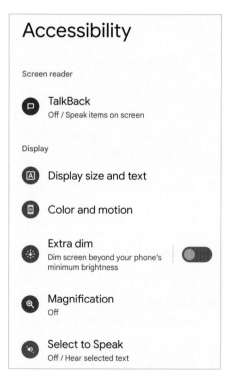

- **Captions**. This can be used for closed captions (subtitles) for videos, TV shows and movies (with compatible apps).

- **Audio**. This category can be used to manage sound issues, including amplifying the sound and using compatible hearing aids with your phone.

...cont'd

Using Accessibility settings

Many of the Accessibility settings have several options for
the required function. For instance, to use the **Display
size and text** option:

1 Tap on the **Display
size and text** option
on the main Accessibility
screen

2 Drag the **Font size**
slider to change the size
of display text, for the
phone's system fonts
and also in any
compatible apps

3 Drag the **Display size** slider to change
the size of app icons on the Home screen

4 Tap the **Bold text**
button **On** to display
system text as bold

5 Tap the **High contrast text** button **On** to create
the best contrast between text and the background

6 Options are previewed at
the top of the screen as
they are applied within
the Accessibility settings

Beware

Not all third-party
apps will support all
of the accessibility
features. Google
apps are most likely
to support a larger
number of them.

Google and Phone Settings

This group of settings can be used to manage your Google Account and also system settings related to the functionality of your phone.

Google

These settings can include:

- **Manage your Google Account**. This can be used to apply a range of settings to your Google Account.

- **Ads**. This can be used to specify how ads are used via your Google Account.

Google

Nick Vandome
nickvandome@googlemail.com

Manage your Google Account

Recommended   All services

Backup is off for photos & videos

1.1 GB of 15 GB (8%) used

Photos & videos aren't being backed up

Manage backup

- **Autofill**. This can be used to enable passwords to be entered automatically on websites.

- **Backup**. This can be used to back up the contents of your Android phone to Google computers (servers) for safekeeping.

- **Devices & sharing**. This can be used to share your phone's screen with other compatible devices – e.g. with a smart TV.

- **Find My Device**. This can be set up to locate your phone if it is lost or stolen.

- **Parental controls**. This can be used to set up restrictions if children or teens are using your phone.

- **Set up & restore**. This can be used to set up a new Android phone or restore one from the details saved in the backup, above.

- **Settings for Google apps**. This has options for managing some of the pre-installed Google apps.

System

These settings can include:

- **Languages & input**. This can be used to set the system language for your phone and default keyboard.

- **Gestures**. This can be used to apply navigation gestures.

- **Date & time**. This can be used to set the phone's internal date and time.

System	
⊕	Languages & input Gboard
⊡	Gestures
⏲	Date & time GMT+00:00 Greenwich Mean Time
☁	Backup
⊡	System update Updated to Android 13

- **Backup**. This can be used to back up the contents of your Android phone, as mentioned on the previous page.

- **System update**. This can be used to check if there is an available update for the phone's operating system – i.e. a new or an updated version of Android.

- **Multiple users**. This can be used to add accounts for other people to use the same device.

- **Reset options**. This can be used to reset various features on the phone, including network settings and a factory reset (erasing all data from the phone).

About

These settings can include:

- **Device name**. This is the default name given to the device. It can be changed by tapping on the name and then entering a new one.

- **Google Account**. This can be used to view details about your Google Account and also synchronize selected items between your phone and your online account.

- **Phone number**. This displays the device's phone number, taken from the SIM card once it has been inserted.

For the **Multiple users** settings, each individual user needs to be signed in separately to their Google Account on the phone.

If you are going to be selling your phone or giving it to someone else, use the **Factory reset** setting in **Reset options**. Otherwise, be careful with this as it will delete all data from the phone.

All Android phones have their own range of **Help** settings, some of which are specific to the manufacturer of the phone.

Quick Settings

While the full range of Android settings can be accessed from the **Settings** app, there is also a **Quick Settings** option that can be accessed from the top of the screen. To use this:

Don't forget

When the Quick Settings panel is first accessed, as in Step 1, the Notifications panel appears below it.

1 Swipe down from anywhere at the top of the screen to access **Quick Settings**

2 Drag down here to expand the **Quick Settings** panel

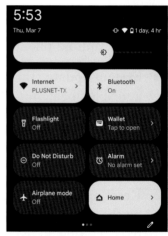

3 Items colored blue are those already active in the **Quick Settings** panel. Tap on other items to activate them too

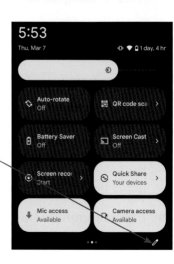

Hot tip

One of the options in the Quick Settings panel is for **Auto-rotate**. If this is **On**, the phone's screen will automatically rotate if you turn it from Portrait mode to Landscape mode. If you want to lock screen rotation, make sure **Auto-rotate** is **Off**.

4 Swipe from right to left to view the full range of **Quick Settings**

5 Tap on this button in the bottom right-hand corner to edit items that appear in the **Quick Settings** panel

3 Around an Android Phone

This chapter details the Android interface and shows how to find your way around the Home screen, add apps and widgets, change the background, and lock your phone. It also covers the sophisticated range of search options that are available, including the digital voice assistant, Google Assistant.

42   Viewing the Home Screen

43   Navigating Around

46   Adding Apps to Home

47   Moving Apps

48   Working with Favorites

49   Creating Folders

50   Adding Widgets

52   Changing the Background

54   Using Notifications

56   Locking Your Phone

58   Searching

60   Google Assistant Search

62   Hey Google

65   Using Google Discover

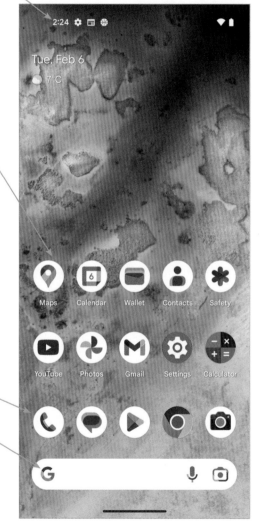

Viewing the Home Screen

Once you have set up your phone, the first screen that you see will be the Home screen. This is also where you will return to when you swipe up from the bottom of the screen (see the next page). Elements of the Home screen include:

Hot tip

Swipe down from anywhere at the top of the screen to view current notifications in the Notifications panel, alongside **Quick Settings**.

Notifications bar

Home screen area. This is where the majority of your commonly used apps and widgets will be located.

Favorites Tray

Google Search box

Swipe up over the apps in the Favorites Tray to access the **All Apps** section, which includes all of the apps on the Android phone.

Navigating Around

The methods of navigating around Android phones have evolved with the development of new devices and new versions of Android. With Android 13, much of the navigation is done by using physical gestures on the phone, although some models may also use the older method of buttons on the body of the phone – see page 45. The navigation options include:

Returning to Home

To return to the Home screen, from any app on your phone, swipe up on the bar at the bottom of the screen. The current window will be replaced by the Home screen.

Most Android phones have several Home screens. Swipe left and right to move between them.

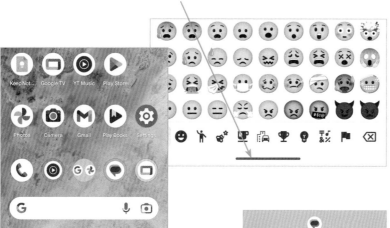

For returning to the Home screen, don't swipe too far up on the screen – the action is a short swipe.

Recent items

To view apps that have been recently used and not closed, swipe up from the bar at the bottom of the screen to the middle of the screen. Swipe left and right on the **Recents** screen to view available open apps. Tap on an app to expand it to full size and make it the active one.

43

...cont'd

Back

When navigating through screens on an Android phone, there are frequent occasions when you want to go back to the previous screen in the app you are using rather than going back to the Home screen. With Android 13, this can be done with a simple gesture. To do this:

Hot tip

The Gestures section (**Settings** > **System** > **Gestures**) is a good place for learning about more gestures to use on your phone and the actions that they can perform.

1 Access a screen within an app that is not the Homepage. In this example, the screen is the **Gestures** section in the **System** category of the **Settings** app

Gestures

Swipe fingerprint for notifications
Off

Quickly open camera
On

Flip camera for selfie
On

System navigation
Gesture navigation

One-handed mode
Off

Hot tip

The **System navigation** option in Step 1 can be used to view the Home, Recents, and Back navigation techniques. There is also a **3-button navigation** option, which displays the three buttons detailed on the next page.

2 To go back one screen, swipe inward from either side of the screen. This takes you back to the previous screen; in this instance, the **System** screen

System

🌐 Languages & input
   Gboard

📱 Gestures

🕐 Date & time
   GMT+00:00 Greenwich Mean Time

☁ Backup

Navigation on older Android phones

Even if older models of Android phones can run
Android 13, they may still have the older method of
navigation with buttons at the bottom of the Home screen:

The navigation buttons are (from right to left):

Back. Tap on this button to go back
to the most recently visited page or screen.

Home. Tap on this button to go back to the most
recently viewed Home screen at any point.

Recent Items. Tap on
this button to view
apps that you have
used most recently:

Tap on one of the
apps to access it again.
Swipe an app to the
top of the screen to
close the app, or tap on
the **Close all** button
to close all currently
open apps.

Newer Android phones
also usually have an
option for showing
these buttons, even if
the default navigation
option is to use
gestures; see the
second Hot tip on the
previous page.

Adding Apps to Home

The Home screen is where you can add and manage apps. To do this:

Don't forget

There are thousands more apps available for downloading from the Play Store. Tap on this button on the Home screen to access the Play Store (see pages 118-123):

Play Store

Hot tip

To remove an app from the Home screen, press and hold on it and drag it to the top of the screen, then place it over the **Remove** button. This only removes it from the Home screen; it does not uninstall it.

46

1 Swipe up from the Google Search box at the bottom of the screen to access the **All Apps** section

2 All of the built-in apps are displayed. Tap on an app to open it

3 To add an app to the Home screen, press and hold on it to view its related options, which can also be done with apps already on the Home screen

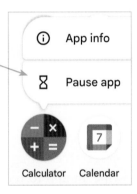

4 Drag the app onto the Home screen to add it

5 Swipe left and right to move between the available Home screens

Moving Apps

Once apps have been added to the Home screen, they can be repositioned and moved to other Home screens. To do this:

1 Press and hold on an app to move it. A light outline appears, indicating that the app can be repositioned

2 Drag the app and release it to drop it into its new position

Don't forget

Apps can be moved to the left or right onto new Home screens, if they are available on either side.

3 To move an app between Home screens, drag it to the edge of the Home screen. As the app reaches the edge of the Home screen, it will automatically move to the next one. Add it to the new Home screen in the same way as in Step 2

Beware

Make sure that the app is fully at the edge of the Home screen; otherwise, it will not move to the next one. A thin, light border should appear just before it moves to the next Home screen.

Working with Favorites

The Favorites Tray at the bottom of the Home screen can be used to access the apps you use most frequently. This appears on all Home screens. Apps can be added to or removed from the Favorites Tray, as required.

Hot tip

Apps can appear in the **Favorites Tray** and also on individual Home screens, but they have to be added there each time from within the **All Apps** section.

Don't forget

When using Android 13 on the Google Pixel smartphone, the Favorites Tray displays suggested apps if there is a space in the Favorites Tray as a result of an app being removed from here. Suggested apps are shown in any available spaces in the Favorites Tray.

1 The apps in the **Favorites Tray** are visible at the bottom of the screen on all Home screens, above the Google Search box

2 Press and hold on an app in the **Favorites Tray** and drag it onto the Home screen to remove it from the Favorites Tray

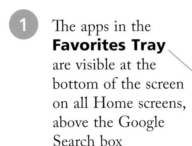

3 Press and hold on an app on the Home screen, and drag it onto a space in the **Favorites Tray** to add it there

4 The **Favorites Tray** has a limit to the number of apps that it can contain, and if you try to add more than this, the app will spring back to its original location

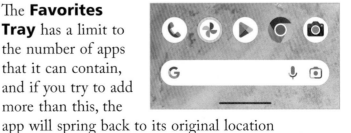
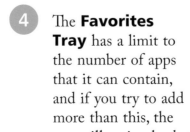

Creating Folders

As you start to use your Android phone for more activities, you will probably acquire more and more apps. These will generally be for a range of tasks covering areas such as productivity, communications, music, photos, and so on. Initially, it may be easy to manage and access these apps, but as the number of them increases, it may become harder to keep track of them all.

One way in which you can manage your apps is to create folders for apps covering similar subjects – e.g. one for productivity apps, one for entertainment apps, etc. To create folders for different apps:

To remove an app from a folder, press and hold on it and drag it out of the folder onto a Home screen.

1 Drag one app over another

2 A folder is created, and the app is added to the folder. Tap here to give the folder a new name

Google   Chrome

Tools

3 Enter the new name for the folder, as required

Google   Chrome

Google Apps

Adding folders to the Favorites Tray is a good way to make a larger number of apps available here.

4 Tap on the folder to open it and view the items within it

Google A...

Adding Widgets

Android widgets are similar to apps, except that they generally display specific content or real-time information. For instance, a photo gallery widget can be used to display photos directly on a Home screen, or a traffic widget can display updated information about traveling conditions. Widgets can be added from any Home screen.

Hot tip

From the panel in Step 1 you can also access wallpapers (see page 52).

1 Press and hold on an empty area on any Home screen and tap on the **Widgets** button

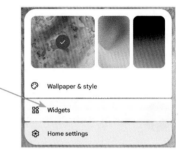

2 Swipe up and down, or sometimes left and right, to view all available widgets

3 Tap on a down-pointing arrowhead in Step 2 to view more details about a widget

4 Press and hold on a widget and drop it onto a Home screen as required, in the same way as for adding apps. Drag the widget icon around the screen to position it

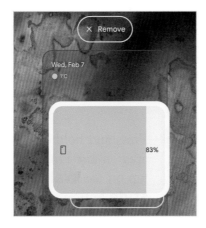

Widget icons on Home screens usually appear larger than those for standard apps.

5 Tap on a widget to view its details. Select options as required, depending on the type of widget

Battery

83 %

About 16 hr, 1 min left

Battery usage
View usage since last full charge

Battery Saver
Off

Adaptive preferences

Battery percentage
Show battery percentage in status bar

6 Press on a widget to access its resizing handles around its border. Drag the handles to resize the widget, as required

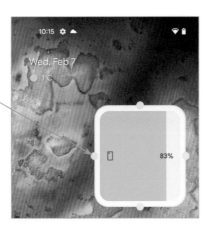

Changing the Background

The background (wallpaper) for all of the Home screens on your phone can be changed within the **Settings** app (**Settings > Wallpaper & style**). However, it can also be changed directly from any Home screen. To do this:

1 Press and hold on an empty area on any Home screen and tap on the **Wallpaper & style** button, or

2 Select **Settings > Wallpaper & style**

3 The current wallpaper for the Lock screen and the Home screen are displayed. Tap on the **Change wallpaper** option

4 Tap on one of the categories for the wallpaper, or tap on the **My photos** option to use your own photos for the wallpaper

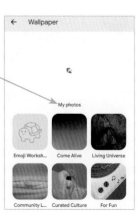

Hot tip

Wallpaper apps can be downloaded from the Play Store to add a wider range of backgrounds to your phone. Enter "**wallpaper**" into the Search box of the **Apps** section of the Play Store.

5 Select an option from one of the categories in Step 4 on the previous page to preview it. Tap on the **Set Wallpaper** button and select to use the wallpaper on the **Lock screen** or the **Home and lock screens**

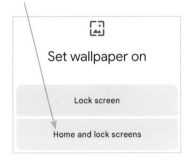

6 Swipe down the page in Step 3 on the previous page and tap the **Themed icons** button **On**

7 The icons on the Home screen are customized to match the wallpaper. If the wallpaper is changed, the customized icons will also change accordingly

Being able to customize the appearance of apps on the Home screen is a new feature in Android 13.

Using Notifications

Android phones have numerous ways of keeping you informed, from new emails and calendar events to the latest information about apps that have been downloaded and installed. To make it easier to view these items, they are grouped together in the Notifications panel. This appears on the Lock screen and can also be accessed from any Home screen by swiping down from the Notifications bar.

1 Notifications are indicated at the top of any Home screen, in the left-hand corner of the Notifications bar

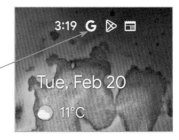

Don't forget

Tap on the **Clear all** button at the bottom of the Notifications panel to clear all current notifications. If you clear notifications it does not delete items; they remain within their relevant apps and can be viewed there.

Clear all

2 Drag down on the Notifications bar to view details of notifications, in the Notifications panel. Tap on a notification to view details about it in its related app

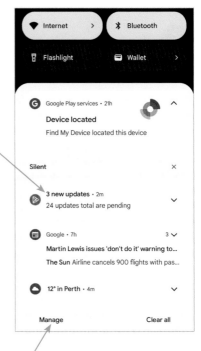

3 Tap on the **Manage** button to access the settings for notifications

Manage

4 Tap on the **App settings** option to specify how notifications operate with specific apps

Tap on the **Notification history** option in Step 4 and drag the **Use notification history** button **On** to view recent notifications and also any that you snoozed when they appeared.

5 Drag the button next to an app **On** or **Off** to enable or disable notifications for the selected app

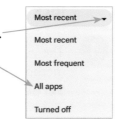

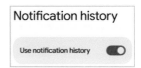

6 Tap here to select which apps are displayed in the Notifications panel. Tap on the **All apps** option to view all of the apps on your phone and specific notification settings, as required

The general settings for notifications can be found within **Settings** > **Notifications**. Swipe up and down to view all of the options.

7 Tap on an app in Step 5 to view further details about it, including the range of notifications used by the app. These individual options can be turned **On** or **Off** within the app, even if the overall setting for the app is different

55

Locking Your Phone

Security is an important issue for any computing device, and this applies to physical security as much as online security. For Android phones, it is possible to place a digital lock on the screen so that only someone who knows the details of the lock can open it. There are different ways in which a lock can be created.

1 Access **Settings** > **Security & privacy**

2 Tap on the **Device lock** option

Device lock
None

3 Tap on the **Screen lock** option

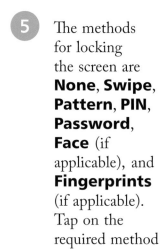

Device lock

Screen lock
None

4 The current method of **Screen lock** is displayed here. Tap on this to access the options

5 The methods for locking the screen are **None**, **Swipe**, **Pattern**, **PIN**, **Password**, **Face** (if applicable), and **Fingerprints** (if applicable). Tap on the required method to select it and set its attributes

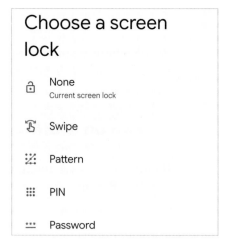

Choose a screen lock

None
Current screen lock

Swipe

Pattern

PIN

Password

Beware

The **Swipe** option is the least secure and is only really useful for preventing items from being activated accidentally when your phone is not in use; it is not a valid security method. The most secure method is a password containing letters, numbers and symbols, or fingerprints.

6 For the **PIN** (or **Password**) option, enter your chosen PIN in the box and tap on the **Next** button. Enter the PIN again for confirmation. This will then need to be entered whenever you want to unlock the phone

PIN stands for Personal Identification Number and is a sequence of numbers chosen by and known only to you.

7 For the **Pattern** option, drag over the keypad to create the desired pattern, repeat to confirm, and this will then be enabled on your Lock screen

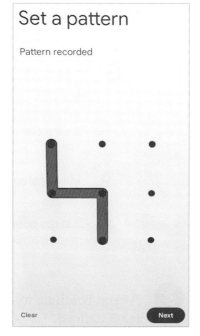

Whenever your phone goes to sleep, it will need to be unlocked before you can use it again. Sleep mode can be activated by pressing the **On/Off** button once. After a period of inactivity it will go into Sleep mode automatically: the length of time until this happens can be specified within **Settings** > **Display** > **Screen timeout**.

57

Searching

Since Android is owned by Google, it is not surprising that phones with this operating system come with the power of Google's search functionality. Items can be searched for within the phone itself, or you can perform searches on the web. This can be done by typing in the Google Search box and also by using the voice search option. To search for items on an Android phone:

1 The Google Search box is usually found on the Home screen, or it can be accessed through the Google app or added via a widget (see pages 50-51)

2 Begin typing a word or phrase. As you type, corresponding suggestions will appear, both for on the web and for apps on the phone (if applicable)

On some phones, the Search option is indicated by a magnifying glass with the word "Google" next to it.

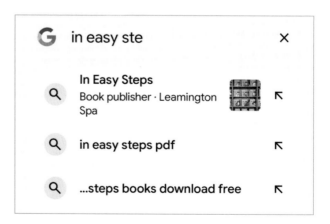

G   in easy ste   ✕

Q   **In Easy Steps**
      Book publisher · Leamington
      Spa

Q   **in easy steps pdf**

Q   **...steps books download free**

3 As you continue to type, the suggestions will become more defined

4 Tap on an app result to open it directly on your phone, or tap on this button on the keyboard to view results from the web

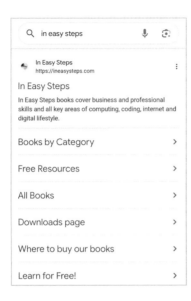

Voice search
To use the voice search functionality on your phone instead of typing a search query:

1 Tap on the microphone button in the Search box

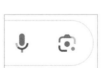

2 When colored dots appear, speak the word or phrase for which you want to search. You can use voice search to find items or open apps (such as the Gmail app) on your phone or search for items on the web

Hot tip

The voice search functionality can also be used for items such as finding directions, setting alarms, and finding photos on your phone.

Don't forget

The phrase displayed in the voice search window is sometimes a summary of what you actually say. For instance, if you say, "Please open Gmail app," the words "open gmail" may be displayed.

Google Assistant Search

One innovation from Google on many Android phones is Google Assistant. This is a personal digital assistant that responds to voice commands. To use Google Assistant:

Once Google Assistant has been set up, it is always available using Hey Google.

1 Set up the "Hey Google" functionality to activate Google Assistant (see pages 62-64)

2 Tap on the **Get Started** button to set up Google Assistant

GET STARTED

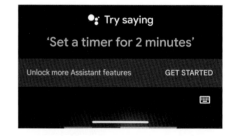

3 Google Assistant offers suggestions for searches based on what is on your screen and also what you have searched for previously

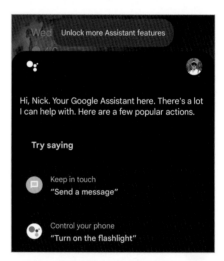

4 Queries can be made of Google Assistant using speech or text options, but speech is easier

...cont'd

5 Speak the query, such as "find the nearest coffee shop"

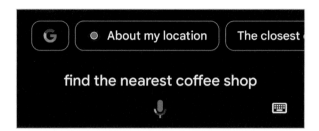

6 Google Assistant displays the results. There are also options for searching for results over the web and viewing them on a map, if applicable

Hot tip

Google Assistant is an excellent option for finding locations when you are traveling. However, this requires a Wi-Fi or cellular network connection, with 3G, 4G or 5G.

Don't forget

Location must be checked **On** (**Settings** > **Location**) for these services to work.

61

Hey Google

Google Assistant incorporates the "Hey Google" functionality, whereby you can use voice search commands from any screen. To set up Hey Google:

62

1. Tap on the **Google** app

2. Tap on the **Account** button

 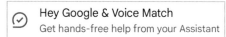

3. Tap on the **Settings** option

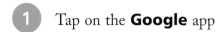

4. Tap on the **Google Assistant** option

5. Tap on the **Hey Google & Voice Match** option

6. If the **Hey Google** button is **Off**, drag it **On** to enable the Assistant when you say "Hey Google" from any screen on your phone

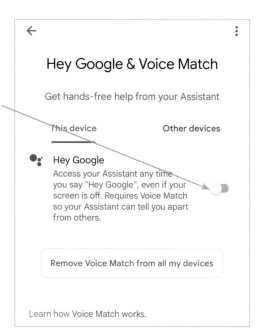

7 Tap on the **More** button at the bottom of the screen

More

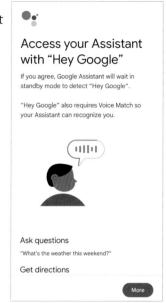

Access your Assistant with "Hey Google"

If you agree, Google Assistant will wait in standby mode to detect "Hey Google".

"Hey Google" also requires Voice Match so your Assistant can recognize you.

Ask questions
"What's the weather this weekend?"

Get directions

More

Once Hey Google is set up you should not have to worry about it again; just use your voice to search for items on your phone.

8 Tap on the **I agree** button to be able to turn off Hey Google in the Assistant settings

You can turn off "Hey Google" in Assistant settings.

No thanks   I agree

9 Tap on the **More** button at the bottom of the screen to enable the Assistant to recognize your voice for using **Hey Google**

More

Teach your Assistant to recognize your voice

Your Assistant will respond when it hears you say "Hey Google" and recognizes your voice.

Voice Match allows your Assistant to identify you and tell you apart from others. The Assistant takes clips of your voice to form a unique voice model, which is only stored on your device(s). Your voice model may be sent temporarily to Google to better identify your voice.

If you decide later that Voice Match isn't for

No thanks   More

...cont'd

Use your normal speaking volume and speed when setting up Hey Google, as this is how you will use the function for everyday use.

10 Follow the on-screen prompts for saying specific phrases. After each one, the circle with the checkmark (tick) is completed, to indicate that step has been successful

Say "Ok Google, what's the weather tomorrow?"

11 At the end of the process, tap on the **Next** button at the bottom of the screen

Next

"Hey Google" is ready

Your device can now recognize your voice when you say "Hey Google" or "Ok Google"

You can change this in voice settings, and view or delete voice commands in your Google activity controls.

Next

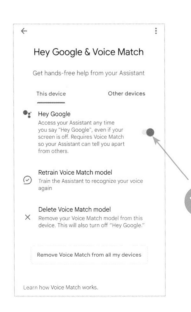

12 The **Hey Google** button is displayed as **On**, indicating that the Assistant will be enabled when you say "Hey Google" from any screen on your phone

Using Google Discover

We live in an age where we want the availability of as much up-to-date information as possible. On an Android phone, one option for this is Google Discover, accessed from the Google app. This is a digital assistant service that can be customized to provide exactly the information you want.

Accessing Google Discover

Google Discover works closely with the Google Assistant and can display a similar range of information. It can be accessed from the Google app.

1 Tap on the **Google** app

2 Tap on the **Discover** button at the bottom of the screen to view the latest news items from Google Discover

3 Tap on the **Menu** button at the right-hand side of the bottom toolbar for an item being viewed to access options for managing it

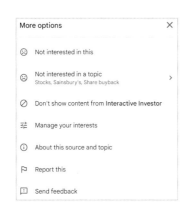

Beware

Google Discover will use information from a variety of your Google searches whenever you are logged in to your Google Account on any device. Therefore, it can take some work with the menu in Step 3 to train Google Discover to display the type of content in which you are most interested.

...cont'd

4 Tap on the **Saved** button on the bottom toolbar

Saved

5 The **Saved** section can include news items for topics you have selected, reminders you have set, shopping list items, and notes you have made

Don't forget

To use Google Discover on your phone, you have to be connected to the internet via Wi-Fi or cellular.

6 Tap on the **Create** button to add new categories to the **Saved** section

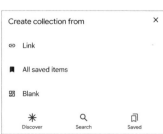

4 Calls and Contacts

This chapter focuses on using an Android phone to make and receive calls, and also how to add details of people who have contacted you.

68 Adding Contacts

70 Saving Contacts from Calls

71 Saving Contacts from Texts

72 Editing Contacts

74 Managing Contacts

76 Making a Call

78 Receiving a Call

81 Setting Ringtones

Adding Contacts

Given the range of uses to which you can put your Android phone, it is sometimes overlooked that one of its original functions is to make phone calls to people. This can be done by typing a number directly into the phone dialer (see page 76). However, it is generally better to first add contacts to your phone, and then you can use these details to keep in touch with them in a variety of ways. To add a contact:

The Contacts option can also be accessed from the **Phone** app, from the Contacts tab.

1 Tap on the **Contacts** app

2 Tap on the **+** button to add a new contact to your Contacts list

3 Select where you want to store the contact. Generally, it is better to store contacts to your Google Account (**Google Contacts**) as this will ensure that they are backed up on Google computers, and you will be able to access them from any online computer or device by logging in to your Google Account. If contacts are only saved to your phone (**Device**), then you may not be able to synchronize them and access them from other devices. Tap on the **Save** button

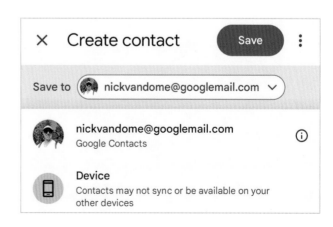

4 Enter details for the new contact and tap on the **Save** button at the top of the screen

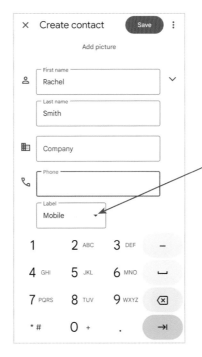

Tap here next to a category to add more options for it – e.g. to add a home phone number and a mobile/ cell phone one too.

5 The new contact is added to the **Contacts** app (which is also accessed from the **Contacts** tab in the **Phone** app)

R   (R)   Rachel Smith

In some locations "Mobile" will appear as "Cellular."

6 Tap on a contact to see their details. Tap on the **Text** icon to create a text message for the selected contact, the phone icon to make a call to them, or the video icon to make a video call

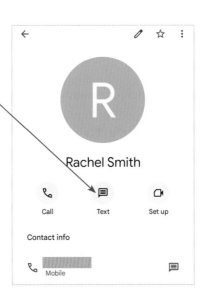

Saving Contacts from Calls

Another quick way to add a contact is to ask someone to phone you so that you can then copy their number directly from your phone to your contacts. You do not even have to answer the phone to do this.

Don't forget

When you receive a call while you are using another app, accept it by tapping on the green button. To reject a call, tap on the red button.

1. Once someone has phoned, tap on the **Phone** button

2. Tap on the **Recents** tab. The call or text will be displayed

3. If the number is not already in your contacts, tap on it

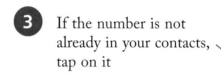

4. Tap on the **Add contact** button

Don't forget

The **Recents** page shows the most recent calls and texts you have received.

5. Select where you want to save the contact in the **Save to** field and enter the required details to add them to the **Contacts** app in the same way as on page 69. Tap on the **Save** button to complete adding the new contact

Saving Contacts from Texts

Contacts can also be saved from text messages.

1 Open the **Messages** app. Tap on the **Conversations** tab and tap on a conversation

Messages

2 If the number is not already in your contacts, tap on it and tap on the **Add contact** button

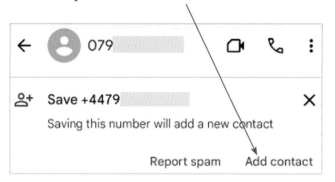

Hot tip

Someone can send you a text just so that you can add their details to your contacts.

3 Select where you want to save the contact in the **Save to** field and enter the required details to add them to the **Contacts** app in the same way as on the previous page

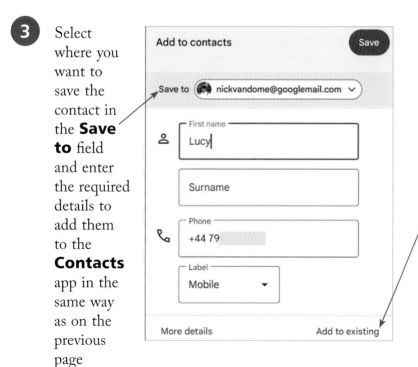

Hot tip

If someone is already in your contacts but you do not have their cell/mobile number included, or you want to update an existing number, tap on **Add to existing** after tapping on **Add contact** in Step 2 to add the number to their existing details.

Editing Contacts

Once contacts have been added to your Android phone you can still edit their details, whether they have been added to the phone or your Google Account. To do this:

1 Tap on the **Contacts** app

2 Access a contact and tap on their name to view their details

3 The current details are displayed. Tap on the **Edit** button on the top toolbar

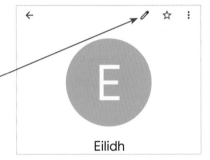

4 Edit the details as required

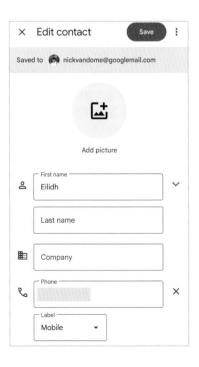

Hot tip

If you have downloaded messaging apps such as WhatsApp, the information from your Contacts list will be synced with this, and any of your contacts who are using the service will automatically be displayed in the messaging app if you agree to this when you install the WhatsApp app.

5 If an image has not been assigned to the contact, tap on the **Add picture** option

Add picture

6 Select an option for assigning an image to the contact, as required

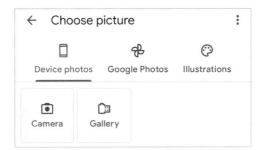

7 Tap on an item's **Label** to view its options

8 Tap on a new label, as required, to add to the selected option

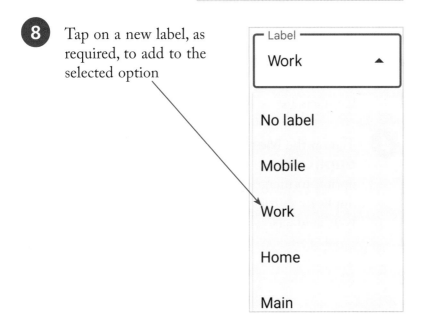

Beware

If a contact has more than one phone number, make sure that you select the required one when phoning or text messaging them.

9 Tap on the **Save** button to confirm any editing changes that have been made

Save

Managing Contacts

Android phones have settings for managing contacts, which include merging duplicate entries and exporting all of your contacts into a single file so that you can send them to friends and family or open them in other apps. To manage your contacts and fix any issues with them:

1 Tap on the **Contacts** app

2 Tap on the **Fix & manage** button at the right-hand side of the bottom toolbar

3 The full range of **Fix & manage** options is listed. Tap on the **Merge & fix** option to merge any duplicate entries and remedy any issues with your Contacts list

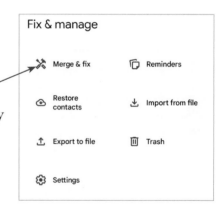

Fix & manage

⚒ Merge & fix   🗐 Reminders

⌾ Restore contacts   ⭳ Import from file

⭱ Export to file   🗑 Trash

⚙ Settings

4 Tap on the **Merge duplicates** option to merge duplicate entries in your contacts

← Merge & fix

Easy ways to fix up your contacts
Get help merging duplicates, adding useful details, and more

Got it

🗐 Merge duplicates
Review 16 people with duplicate listings

👤 Keep contacts up to date
Found new details for 1 person you've contacted

Don't forget

Duplicate entries can be created if you enter contacts on different devices or online with your Google Account.

Don't forget

Keep contacts up-to-date when you are informed that someone has a new phone number or email address.

5 All duplicate entries are displayed. Tap on the **Merge** button to merge an individual entry, or tap on the **Merge all** button for all duplicates

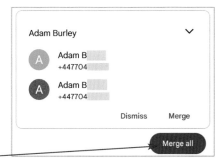

Exporting and importing contacts

To export your contacts into a single file and import them from the same type of file:

1 Tap on **Export to file** in Step 3 on the previous page

> **Don't forget**
>
> VCF stands for Virtual Contact File, which is a text file format for contacts. Once contacts have been exported, they can be shared with other people, using the .vcf file format in Step 2.

2 All of the entries in the Contacts app are included in the **contacts.vcf** file. Tap on the **Save** button to save the file

3 To import contacts, tap on **Import from file** in Step 3 on the previous page and select where you want to store the imported file – i.e. within your Google Account or on your phone

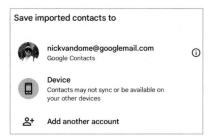

> **Don't forget**
>
> The **Downloads** folder (where the .vcf file is placed once it has been exported) is located within the **Files** app. The **Files** app is a Google app, and if it is not already on your phone, it can be downloaded from the Play Store.

Making a Call

Once you have added contacts to your phone, there are different ways in which you can phone them.

Typing a number

You can make a call by accessing the phone dialer and typing a contact's number on the keypad. To do this:

1 Tap on the **Phone** app

2 Tap on the **Keypad** button at the bottom of the screen. Type the person's number on the keypad. As the number is entered, corresponding names will be displayed from your Contacts list

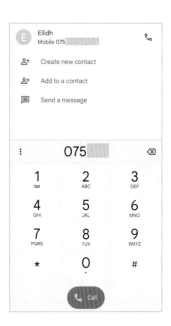

Calls can also be made to people who are not in your contacts, by entering the required number and tapping on the **Call** button in Step 4.

3 Tap on the contact's name to display the full range of available options

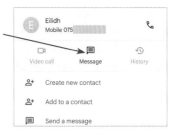

4 Tap on the **Call** button to call the number

Searching for a contact

Once you have added contacts to your Contacts list, you can access them and then call them. To do this:

1   Tap on the **Phone** app

2   Tap on the **Contacts** tab. At the top of the Contacts list is a Search box

Contacts

3   Tap in the **Search contacts** box

≡   Search contacts   ⋮   👤

4   Start typing a name you want to find. All matching results are shown. The more characters of a name that you type, the more the search results will be narrowed down. Tap on the **Call** button to call the contact

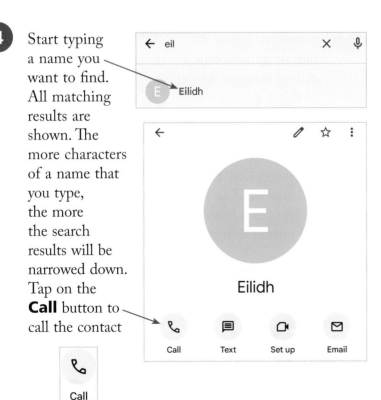

Hot tip

On some models of Android phone it is possible to place a call to a contact in your Contacts list, just using one swipe. To do this, access the Contacts list and swipe from left to right on a contact's name. A **Call** button appears and the call is connected automatically. Swipe from right to left on a contact's name to send them a text message rather than make a call.

Receiving a Call

When you receive a call, the caller's name will show up on the screen (if they are in your contacts), accompanied by a ringtone (see pages 81-82).

Hot tip

On some Android models, if the caller has sent you any text messages, the latest one will be displayed on the **Incoming call** screen.

Hot tip

Tap on the **Message** button in Step 1 to reject the call but send the caller a text message instead.

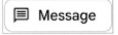

1 When a call is received, the caller's name is displayed (if they have been added as a contact) along with their phone number. If their photo has been added to their contact details, this will be displayed too

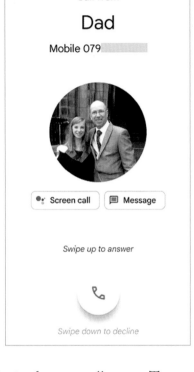

2 Swipe the green button up to accept a call, or swipe it down to reject it

3 If you are using another app when a call is received, the full-size window is minimized to a smaller one. Tap on the green button to accept the call, or tap on the red button to reject it

4 Once a call has been accepted, these buttons appear at the bottom of the window, when in full-screen mode

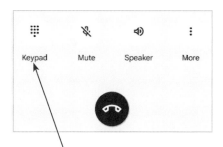

5 Tap on the **Keypad** button to access a keypad that can be used during the call – i.e. if you are selecting options during an automated call

Don't forget

The hash key (#) on the keypad is frequently requested when making selections during automated calls.

6 Tap on the **Speaker** button to activate the speaker so that you can hear the call without holding the phone to your ear

7 The Home screen, or other apps, can be accessed during a call by pressing the **Home** button (or by swiping up from the bottom of the screen on newer phones), in which case the call icon is minimized at the top of the screen

13:39

...cont'd

8 During a call in full-screen mode, tap on the **More** button at the top of the call window

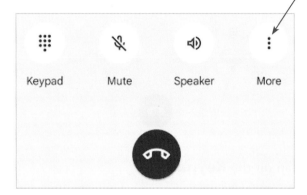

9 Select options for the call, including **Hold**, to put the current call on hold so that the other person is still on the call but cannot hear you; **Video call**, to convert an audio call to a video one; and **Add call**, to add more people to an existing call

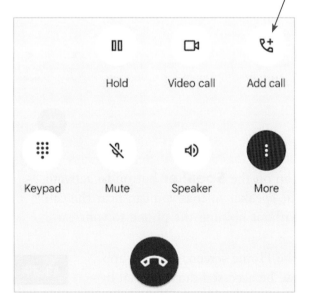

Don't forget

Google's video-chatting app was previously known as Duo. It is now the **Meet** app.

10 Tap on the red **End call** button to end the current call

Setting Ringtones

Ringtones were one of the original must-have accessories that helped transform the way people looked at mobile/cell phones. Android phones have a range of ringtones that can be used, and you can also download and install thousands more. To use the default ringtones:

1 Tap on the **Settings** app

Settings

2 Tap on the **Sound & vibration** button

🔊 **Sound & vibration**
Volume, haptics, Do Not Disturb

3 Tap on one of the **Phone ringtone** options for ringtones for when you receive a phone call

Phone ringtone
The Big Adventure

4 Tap on one of the options to hear a preview

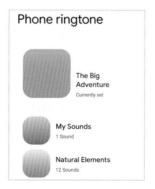

5 With the desired tone selected, tap on the **Save** button to select a ringtone for your phone

...cont'd

Getting more ringtones

While the default ringtones will serve a perfectly good purpose, there is also a wealth of sounds and music that can be downloaded and used as ringtones. This can be done through the Google Play Store.

Beware

Experimenting with different ringtones can be good fun, but after a while you may find that they can become slightly irritating for you and those nearby.

1 Access the Google Play Store app. Tap on the Search box and enter **ringtones** to see the available options

Play Store

2 Tap on one of the search results

3 Tap on one of the ringtone apps to download it

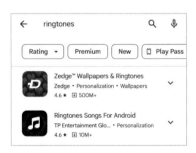

4 Tap on the download icon to complete the download process

5 Once the ringtone app has been downloaded, tap on it to open it and select options for how it operates

5 Using the Keyboard

This chapter looks at entering text and data with the keyboard on an Android phone, focusing on the widely available Google keyboard: Gboard.

84 Keyboards with Android

85 Selecting Keyboards

86 About the Google Keyboard

88 Keyboard Settings

90 Gboard Suggestion Strip

92 General Keyboard Shortcuts

93 Adding Text

94 Working with Text

Keyboards with Android

All Android phones have a keyboard for inputting text and data, and the vast majority of them are virtual ones – i.e. they appear on the screen rather than an actual physical keyboard. Different phone manufacturers add their own keyboards to their specific handsets, and this is usually the default keyboard that appears. However, different keyboards can be downloaded from the Play Store, including the Google keyboard (Gboard), which is a good, multi-purpose Android keyboard. To download different keyboards:

As the Google keyboard is produced by Google, it can be considered the default Android keyboard and is used for the examples in this chapter.

1 Access the Play Store and type **android keyboard** into the Search box

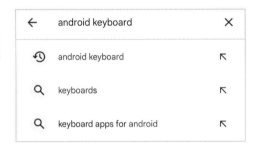

2 Tap on one of the search results to view the keyboard app and download and install it, if required

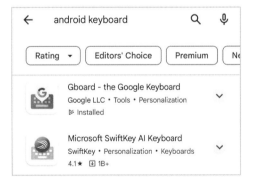

3 The keyboard app will be added to the next available Home screen. Tap on it to set it up and also access its settings once setup is completed

Selecting Keyboards

Several different keyboards can be installed and used on your Android phone. Keyboards can be changed at any time and different ones selected. To do this:

1 Tap on **Settings** and select **System**

System
Languages, gestures, time, backup

2 Tap on the **Languages & input** option

System

Languages & input
Gboard

3 Tap on the **On-screen keyboard** option

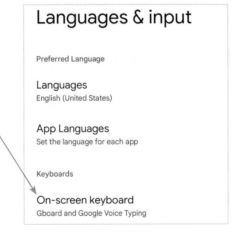
Languages & input

Preferred Language

Languages
English (United States)

App Languages
Set the language for each app

Keyboards

On-screen keyboard
Gboard and Google Voice Typing

Don't forget

Most Android phone manufacturers include their own keyboards on their phones and these are the default ones that are used, until a different one is selected.

4 The available keyboards are listed. Tap on one to view its details and select it as the default

On-screen keyboard

Gboard
Multilingual typing

Google Voice Typing
Automatic

Microsoft SwiftKey Keyboard
Microsoft SwiftKey Keyboard

About the Google Keyboard

As with other Android keyboards, the Google keyboard (Gboard) can be used for a variety of actions:

- Entering text with a messaging app, word processing app, email app or a notes app.

- Entering a web address.

- Entering information into a form.

- Entering a password.

Viewing the keyboard

When you attempt one of the tasks above, the keyboard appears before you can enter any text or numbers:

When using the keyboard for normal text or data entry, it only requires a light touch; you do not have to press very hard on the keys.

The **Numbers** bar on the Gboard is permanently available as part of the top row of letters. Press and hold on a letter to add the number above it.

Caps Lock means that all letters will be entered as capital letters.

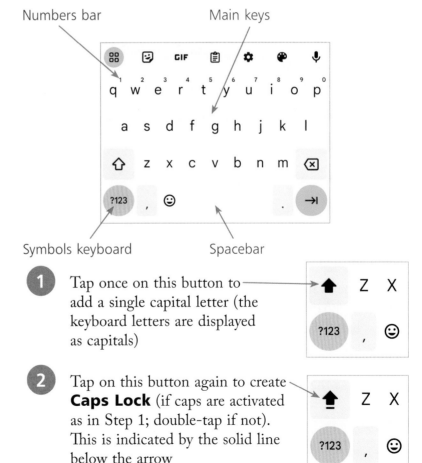

Numbers bar   Main keys

Symbols keyboard   Spacebar

1 Tap once on this button to add a single capital letter (the keyboard letters are displayed as capitals)

2 Tap on this button again to create **Caps Lock** (if caps are activated as in Step 1; double-tap if not). This is indicated by the solid line below the arrow

3 Tap once on this button to back-delete an item

4 Tap once on this button to access the **Symbols** keyboard option

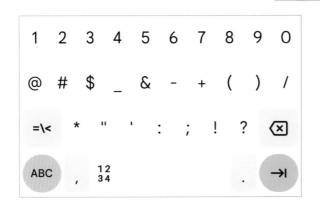

5 Tap on this button to access the second page of the **Symbols** keyboard

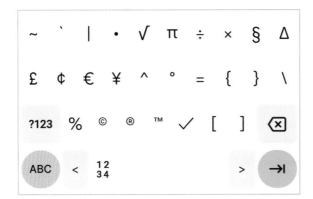

6 Tap once on this button on either of the **Symbols** keyboards above to return to the standard **QWERTY** option

Hot tip

Tap on this button to access the number pad for entering numerical data:

12
34

Don't forget

Sometimes, the button in Step 5 is **1/2** or **2/2**. Tap these buttons to move between the **Symbols** pages.

Hot tip

If you are entering a password, or details into a form, the keyboard will have a **Go** or **Send** button that can be used to activate the information that has been entered.

Keyboard Settings

There are a number of options for setting up the functionality of the Google keyboard.
These can be accessed in two ways:

Don't forget

Tap on the **Preferences** button in Step 3 to access a range of options for the keys on the keyboard, and layout and key press options such as for sounds and vibrations for when keys are pressed.

1 Tap on the **Gboard** app; or

2 Tap on the **Settings** button on the top shortcuts bar of the Google keyboard

3 A full list of keyboard settings is displayed

4 Tap on the **Languages** option to select different languages

5 Tap on the **Theme** option to select a colored theme for the keyboard

6 Tap on the **Dictionary** option for creating a personal dictionary that lets you add your own words to the dictionary, and also shortcuts for frequently used words or names

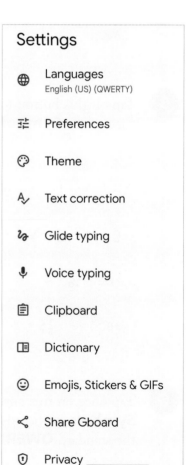

Settings

🌐 Languages
English (US) (QWERTY)

⇌ Preferences

🎨 Theme

A Text correction

ぬ Glide typing

🎤 Voice typing

📋 Clipboard

▥ Dictionary

☺ Emojis, Stickers & GIFs

⮜ Share Gboard

🛡 Privacy _____

Don't forget

Most keyboards have a **Predictive text** setting. This is a function where words are suggested as you type them: as more letters are added to a word, the suggestions becomes more defined. In the Gboard app, this functionality is provided by the **Show suggestion strip** option (see the next page).

7 Tap on the **Text correction** button on the previous page, to access options for working with text as it is being written

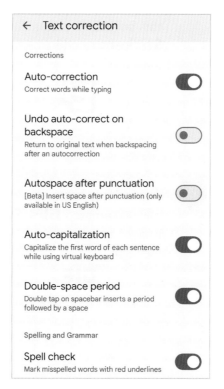

Text correction

Suggestions

Show suggestion strip
Display suggestion strip while typing

Next-word suggestions
Use previous words in making suggestions

Block offensive words
Do not suggest potentially offensive words

Suggest Contacts
Use information from Contacts for suggestions

Smart Compose

Corrections

The **Show suggestion strip** option in Step 8 displays suggested words as you type (tap on one to select it); **Next-word suggestions** displays a possible next word, based on the one just used; and **Suggest Contacts** displays names from the Contacts app.

8 Drag **On** or **Off** the buttons for **Show suggestion strip**, **Next-word suggestions**, **Block offensive words**, and **Suggest Contacts**

9 Scroll down the **Text correction** page to access options for **Auto-correction**, **Undo auto-correct on backspace**, **Autospace after punctuation**, **Auto-capitalization**, **Double-space period**, and **Spell check**. Drag the buttons **On** or **Off** as required to apply or disable the settings

← Text correction

Corrections

Auto-correction
Correct words while typing

Undo auto-correct on backspace
Return to original text when backspacing after an autocorrection

Autospace after punctuation
[Beta] Insert space after punctuation (only available in US English)

Auto-capitalization
Capitalize the first word of each sentence while using virtual keyboard

Double-space period
Double tap on spacebar inserts a period followed by a space

Spelling and Grammar

Spell check
Mark misspelled words with red underlines

The **Auto-correction** option lets you insert the currently highlighted word by tapping on the spacebar; **Auto-capitalization** automatically inserts a capital letter at the start of a new sentence; **Double-space period** adds a period/full stop when the spacebar is tapped twice.

Gboard Suggestion Strip

At the top of the Gboard keyboard (and most other Android keyboards) is the Suggestion strip, if **Show suggestion strip** is turned on – see Step 8 on page 89. This can be used to display next-word suggestions (see page 93) and also add a range of content.

1 Tap on this button to expand the Suggestion strip – see Step 8 on the next page

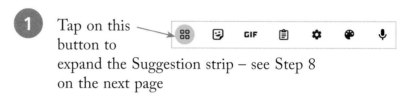

2 Tap on this button to minimize the Suggestion strip

Voice typing can also be accessed from the Suggestion strip by tapping on this button:

(See page 101 for details.)

3 From the expanded Suggestion strip, tap on this button to access **Stickers** to add to a message

4 Tap on this button to select animated **GIF** images to add to a message

5 Tap on this button to access the **Clipboard**, where items have been copied to the clipboard so that they can be pasted into a message. Tap on the **Turn on Clipboard** button if this is not already **On**

 Copy more for faster pasting

Gboard's clipboard lets you copy text and images, keeping them for 1 hour, to quickly paste many things at once.

Turn on Clipboard

6 Tap on this button to access the **Gboard** settings

7 Tap on this button to select color themes to be applied within the app being used

8 Additional options include: using the keyboard **One-handed**; **Text editing**; **Share Gboard** with someone else; **Translate**; **Floating**, which enables the keyboard to be moved around the screen; **Resize**, for resizing the keyboard; and **Emoji**, for adding emojis to text

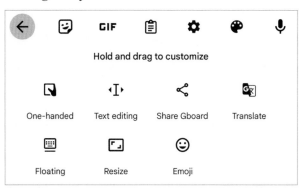

← 😊 GIF 📋 ⚙ 🎨 🎤

Hold and drag to customize

One-handed   Text editing   Share Gboard   Translate

Floating   Resize   Emoji

Hot tip

If the **One-handed** option is selected in Step 8, the keyboard can be moved to the left or the right of the screen so that it can more easily be accessed using just one hand.

91

Don't forget

For some items on the Suggestion strip, such as **Translate**, an item of text has to be selected for it to be active.

General Keyboard Shortcuts

Because of the size of the keyboard on an Android phone, some keys have duplicate functionality in order to fit in all of the options. This includes dual-function keys, spacebar shortcuts, and accented letters.

Much of this functionality is accessed by pressing and holding on the keys, rather than just tapping on them once.

Dual functions

If a key has more than one character, both items can be accessed from the same button.

1 Press and hold on the period/full stop key to view additional options. Slide your finger over a character to insert it

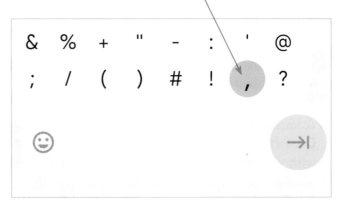

Hot tip

Press and hold on compatible letters on the keyboard to access accented versions for different languages. These include the a, c, e, i, o, s and u keys.

Spacebar shortcut

The spacebar can also be used for a useful shortcut: at the end of a sentence, double-

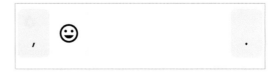

tap on the spacebar to add a full stop/period and a space, ready for the start of the next sentence if this is enabled as shown in Step 9 on page 89.

The end.|

Adding Text

Once you have applied the keyboard settings that you require, you can start entering text in appropriate apps.

1 Tap once in a text box to activate the keyboard. Start typing with the keyboard. Text will appear at the point where you tapped on the screen

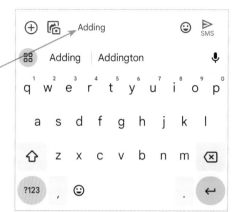

Use the back-delete button to remove unwanted text once it has been added.

2 If **Show suggestion strip** is enabled, suggestions appear above the keyboard as you type a word. Tap once on a word on the Suggestion strip to include it, or continue typing to ignore suggestions

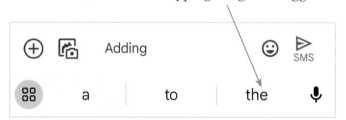

If **Show suggestion strip** is enabled in the keyboard settings (see page 89), **Next-word suggestions** is automatically enabled.

3 If **Next-word suggestions** is enabled, suggestions appear after the last word entered

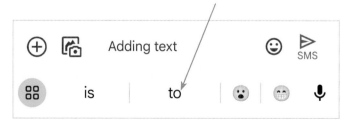

For details about adding text to a text message, see pages 96-97.

Working with Text

Once text has been entered, it can be selected, copied, cut and pasted, either within an app or between apps.

Selecting text

To select text and perform tasks on it:

1 Tap anywhere to set an insertion point for adding or editing text

2 Drag the marker to move an insertion point

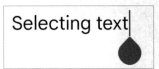

3 Double-tap or press and hold on a word to select it and activate the selection handles

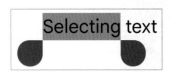

4 Drag the handles to change text that is selected

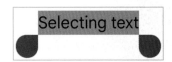

Don't forget

To select all of the text in a text box, press and hold on the text, then tap on the **Select all** button in Step 6.

5 Tap on these options to cut or copy selected text

6 Locate the point at which you want to insert text, and press and hold. Tap on **Paste** to add the text

6 Messaging and Email

This chapter shows how to keep in touch using text messages and how to enhance them with emojis and attachments.

96 Texting Contacts

98 Using Emojis

100 Adding Attachments

101 Sending a Voice Note

102 Setting Up Email

104 Using Gmail

106 Going Hands-free

When you send a text message to someone, this starts a conversation thread. To delete a thread in the **Messages** app, press and hold on the conversation thread and tap on the **Trash** icon at the top of the window.

Don't forget

Apps such as **WhatsApp** and **Messenger** (Facebook) can be used for texting people. This is known as "internet messaging," and one of its useful features is being able to create text groups so that everyone in a group can see what the other members are saying. It is usually free to message people with these apps. The **Messages** app on your Android phone can also create groups.

Texting Contacts

As with phone calls, it is possible to use your contacts to send text messages in different ways.

Finding a contact in Messages

To text a contact directly from the Messages app:

1 Tap on the **Messages** app

2 Tap on the **Start chat** button

3 Enter details of a recipient and tap on one of the options that appear, as required

4 Enter text for the message

Texting with Eilidh (SMS/MMS)

> Hi, how's it going?

5 Compose the text and tap on this button to send the message

...cont'd

Texting from your Contacts list

You can also text a contact directly from your Contacts list.

1 Tap on the **Contacts** app

Contacts

2 Find the contact you want to text

3 Tap on the contact's name and tap on the **Text** icon. A new text message is opened with the contact's name already inserted

Text

Don't forget

To call a contact instead of sending them a text, tap on the **Call** button (to the left of the **Text** button).

97

Quick contact messaging

On some models of Android phones, it is possible to quickly start a text message with a contact with one swipe.

1 Tap on the **Contacts** app

Contacts

2 Find the contact you want to text

3 Swipe to the left on the contact's name. A blue  **Message** button appears and opens up a new text message with the contact's name already inserted as the recipient

Beware

When you are accessing a contact's details by tapping on their name, be careful not to swipe the button instead, as this could activate the quick messaging or calling function by mistake.

Using Emojis

Emojis (small graphical symbols) are now a common sight in text messages and on social media. Some people love them, while others loathe them, but they are now a regular feature in digital communications.

Emojis can be inserted directly from the **Messages** text box.

Beware

Use emojis sparingly, as the novelty can soon wear off for the recipient.

Hot tip

Emojis can also be added to emails and any apps where the emoji keyboard is available.

1 Compose a text message, and at any point, tap on the emoji symbol on the keyboard

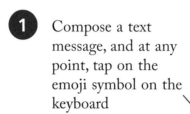

2 The default category of emojis is displayed. Tap on an item to add it to a message

3 Tap on this button to view the most recently used emojis

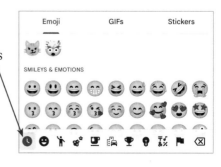

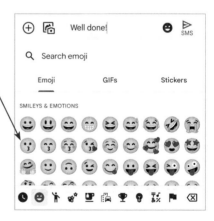

4 Tap on the buttons on the bottom toolbar to view the emojis' different categories

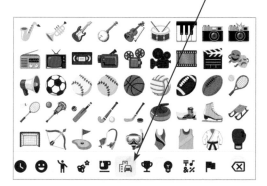

The range of emojis on the Gboard app has been updated for Android 13.

5 Swipe left and right or tap on the buttons below the emojis to view the emojis in a category. Tap on an emoji to add it

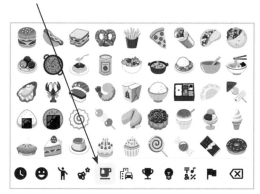

6 When writing a message, emojis will appear on the Suggestion strip when they match a word that has been entered. Tap on an emoji to replace the word

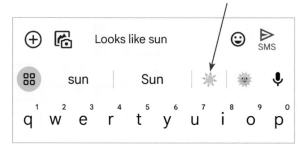

Adding Attachments

Text messages do not have to only include words; it is also possible to attach a variety of other items, such as photos, documents, and even your current location. To do this:

Beware

If a photo or video is too large to be sent by text, you will see a message saying that it will be compressed before it can be sent.

1 Open a new text message and tap on this button next to the text box

2 Tap on the category of item to be added – e.g. an image, stickers, or a map location

3 Make a selection from the category selected in Step 2. The item is included with the text message when it is sent

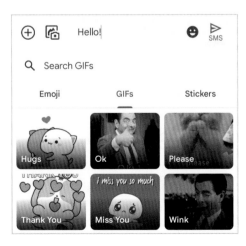

Sending a Voice Note

The Messages app can be used to send recorded voice messages, known as voice notes. To do this:

1 Tap on the **Messages** app, in the same way as for creating a text message

2 Press and hold on the microphone icon at the right-hand side of the text box to start recording a voice note

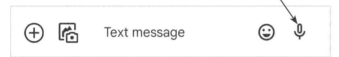

Text message

3 Speak clearly into the phone to record the message. The timer at the left-hand side displays the duration of the message

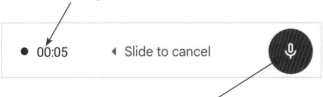

● 00:05 ◀ Slide to cancel

4 Release the microphone icon to finish the message. The voice note is added to the text box. Additional text can be added, if required, but this is optional. Tap on the **Send** button to send the message, with the voice note within it

00:06

Hi, this voice note says it all!

MMS

Don't forget

Voice notes are an increasingly popular method of communication, so be prepared to see more of them appearing in your messaging apps.

Don't forget

Email accounts can also be set up from the **Settings** app, under **Passwords & accounts** > **Add account**.

Hot tip

Usually, email providers have their own apps – e.g. **Microsoft Outlook** for Microsoft accounts; **Yahoo Mail** for Yahoo accounts; etc.

Setting Up Email

Email is still one of the main forms of electronic communication. Most Android phone manufacturers include their own email app for adding email accounts, but the **Gmail** app can also be used for this, in addition to being used for emails from a Google Account. To add an email account:

1. Tap on the **Gmail** app

2. Tap on the Gmail **Menu** button in the top left-hand corner

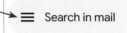

3. Swipe down the menu and tap on the **Settings** button

4. Tap on the **Add account** option to add a new account that can be used with the Gmail app

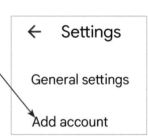

5. Tap on the type of account that you want to add. Tap on the **Other** option if your email account provider is not on the list

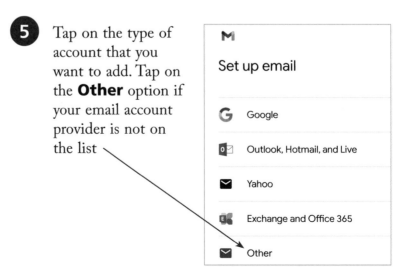

6 Enter the email address of the account you want to add, and then tap on the **Next** button

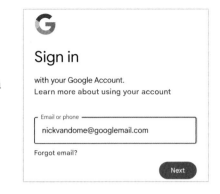

Numerous email accounts can be added to the Gmail app.

7 Enter the password for the account you want to add, and then tap on the **Next** button

When an email account is synced, any items that are saved online are copied to the phone so that the two locations display the same information.

8 Select options for the account, including those for notifications when emails arrive; syncing the account; and downloading attachments. Tap on the **Accept** button to finish setting up the new account

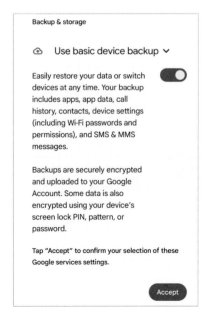

Using Gmail

Accessing emails

Emails from different email accounts can all be viewed and managed using Gmail. To do this:

1   Tap on the **Gmail** app

2   By default, Gmail should open at your Inbox, with your emails displayed. Tap on one to open it. Tap on the **Menu** button to view the mailbox options

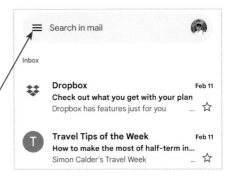

3   Tap on the **Inbox** button to return to your Inbox at any point. Tap on the other options to view folders with specific items, such as **Sent** mail and any **Drafts** you have written

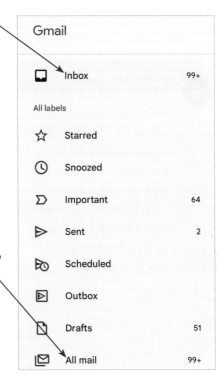

4   Tap on the **All mail** option to view emails from multiple accounts, if more than one has been added to the Gmail app

104

Creating an email

Once you have set up an email account, you can use it to send and receive all emails on your Android phone. To send an email:

1 Tap on the **Gmail** app

2 Tap on the **Compose** button

3 Compose an email by adding a recipient, subject, and body text

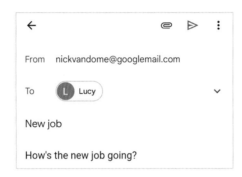

From   nickvandome@googlemail.com

To   L Lucy

New job

How's the new job going?

If a recipient is in your **Contacts** app, their full email address will appear as you type their name in Step 3, provided the email address is included in their entry in the **Contacts** app.

4 To format text, press on a word to select it. Tap on the **Format** button to access the formatting toolbar

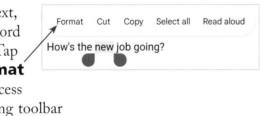

Format   Cut   Copy   Select all   Read aloud

How's the new job going?

5 Choose the required formatting for the selected word, including bold, italics, underlining, text color, background text color, and strikethrough

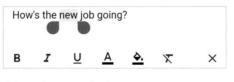

How's the new job going?

B *I* <u>U</u> A ◆. ✕ ✕

Tap on the **Attach** button on the top bar to include photos, video or music files in your email.

6 When you have finished composing your email, tap on this button to send it

105

Going Hands-free

If you do not want to bother fiddling around with fingers and thumbs to create your messages, you can use speech mode instead.

To dictate a message, make sure you use the microphone icon directly above the keyboard, not the one in the text box, which creates a voice note – see page 101.

Creating text with the microphone is not an exact science, and you may find that you end up with some strange interpretations of your words.

1 Open a new text message or email and tap on the microphone icon

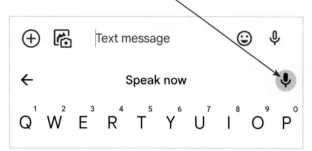

2 When the **Speak now** window appears, speak your message as clearly as possible

3 As you are speaking, the **Listening...** window appears

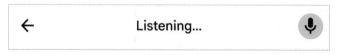

4 Your words will be converted into text

7 Android Apps

The functionality on an Android phone is provided by its apps. This chapter details the pre-installed ones and shows how to download more and update them. It also looks at some of the most common apps, covering maps, notes, social media, health and fitness, and games.

108 Apps for Android

110 Google Apps

112 Maps

114 Notes and Memos

115 Social Media

116 Health and Fitness

117 Playing Games

118 Around the Play Store

120 Finding Apps

122 Downloading Apps

124 Uninstalling Apps

126 Updating Apps

128 App Information

Apps for Android

An app is just a more modern name for a computer program. The terminology first became widely used on smartphones but has now spread to all forms of computing and is firmly embedded in the language of phones.

On Android phones, there are three main types of apps:

- **Generic apps** – Come pre-installed on your Android phone. In general, these apps are specific to the manufacturer of the phone.

- **Google apps** – Downloaded from the online Play Store. Google apps are compatible with the same apps on other Google devices. A number of these apps are also pre-installed on a lot of Android phones.

- **Apps from other developers** – Non-Google apps, downloaded from the Play Store.

Generic apps

The types of generic apps that are available on Android phones include:

- **Calculator**. A standard calculator that also has some scientific functions, although not the range of a full scientific calculator.

Calculator

- **Calendar**. An app for storing appointments, important dates, and other calendar information.

Calendar

- **Camera**. Android smartphones have at least one camera, and most have two: a front-facing and back-facing one. These can be accessed from the **Camera** app.

Camera

- **Clock**. This can be used to view the time in different countries, and also functions as an alarm clock, a timer, and a stopwatch.

Clock

Because of the open source nature of Android, manufacturers can customize the pre-installed apps for their devices.

Most apps have menu options that can be accessed from the buttons below (some apps have both, but they provide the same menu functionality):

- **Contacts**. The **Contacts** app serves as an address book where you can enter details about your friends and family members. Calls and texts can be sent directly from the app.

Contacts

- **Gallery**. In addition to the **Camera** app, some Android phones have a **Gallery** app that can be used to view, manage, edit, and share photos, and other models feature a **Photos** app, which serves the same purpose.

Gallery

- **Internet**. Although a generic internet app is included with a lot of Android phones, the **Google Chrome** app is probably the best option for accessing the web.

Internet

- **Messages**. This is the generic app for sending text messages, which is done through your 3G/4G/5G cellular network.

Messages

- **Phone**. This is the generic app for making calls (and accessing contacts for calls) and video calls.

Phone

- **Play Store**. Although this is a Google app, it is included on most Android phones so that you can access the Play Store for downloading apps, books, music, movies, and magazines.

Play Store

- **Notes/Memos**. Notes and memo apps are provided on most Android phones, and they are useful for jotting down items such as shopping lists and packing lists for traveling.

Notes

- **Settings**. This contains all of the settings that can be applied to the phone so that you can customize it the way you want.

Settings

Health and fitness apps record details including number of steps taken, calories consumed, heart rate, and workout activity. See page 116 for details.

In addition to the Play Store, some phone manufacturers also offer their own app stores, although the range of apps is usually more limited.

Google Apps

Most Android phones come with some Google apps already pre-installed. If not, the apps can be downloaded from the Play Store. The Google apps for Android phones include:

110

- **Assistant**. This is Google's app for searching for items by speaking. Tap on the app and then speak your search query.

Assistant

- **Chrome**. Different Android phones have different types of browsers for accessing the web. The Chrome browser is the default on some phones.

Chrome

- **Docs**. This can be used to create word processing documents and keep them in cloud storage (online storage) or on your phone.

Docs

- **Drive**. This app provides online storage and backup for documents and files on your phone, stored by Google.

Drive

- **Gmail**. When you set up a Google Account, you will also create a Gmail account for sending and receiving email. This app can be used for accessing and using your Gmail.

Gmail

- **Google**. This app can be used for accessing the **Google Search** function – still one of the best search facilities available. It can also be used for accessing the **Google Discover** function.

Google

- **Google TV**. Google TV has replaced the **Google Play Movies & TV** app, and offers a huge range of movies and TV shows.

Google TV

- **Maps**. The Google Maps app is one of the best mapping apps available for finding locations and obtaining directions.

Maps

- **Meet**. This is Google's app for making video calls, using your Google Account and your device's camera.

Meet

- **News**. This is a news app that collates stories on specific topics or from certain publications.

News

Don't forget

Some Android phones have different apps for functions such as playing music and movies, and reading books and magazines. If this is the case, the Play apps here can still be downloaded from the Play Store.

- **Play Books**. This is an app for reading ebooks on an Android phone. It can be used to manage books in your library and also download new ones from the Play Store.

Play Books

- **Play Games**. This is an app for accessing games from the Play Store and playing them on your phone.

Play Ga...

- **Sheets**. This can be used to create spreadsheets and keep them in cloud storage (online storage) or on your phone.

Sheets

- **Slides**. This can be used to create presentations and keep them in cloud storage (online storage) or on your phone.

Slides

- **YouTube**. This is the popular video-sharing app that is now owned by Google. It can be used to view millions of videos covering most subjects imaginable.

YouTube

- **YT Music**. **YouTube Music** (**YT Music**) has replaced the **Play Music** app that was previously available on Android smartphones. A huge range of music can be accessed from here.

YT Music

Don't forget

When viewing a map in Step 2, tap on this button (further down the screen) to view your current location at any point:

Maps

The default maps app on Android phones is **Google Maps**, one of the best mapping apps on the market. It can be used to view locations, get directions, and view transit details.

1 Tap on the **Maps** app

Maps

2 The current location is displayed (if **Location** is enabled under **Settings > Location**). Double-tap with one finger to zoom in; double-tap with two fingers to zoom out. Swipe outward with thumb and forefinger to zoom in; pinch inward to zoom out

3 To view other locations, type a place name, address, zip/postcode or landmark in the Search box at the top of the window. Results are displayed as you type

4 Tap on one of the results to view a map of it. Some locations also have additional features such as photos. Tap on an item to view it, or swipe up from the bottom of the window to view more details about a location and questions that have been asked about it

Getting directions

The **Maps** app is very effective in providing directions between two points. To use this functionality:

1 Once you have searched for the destination location as shown on the previous page, tap on the **Directions** button

2 Enter the starting point at the top of the window (by default, the starting point is your current location, but this can be changed by tapping in the field and entering a new location for the starting point). The route is displayed on the map. Tap the **Menu** button to add a stop, and for more options

3 Tap on these buttons to select a mode of transport for the journey

4 Tap on the **Start** button to view step-by-step directions for the journey

5 As you change your location, the map updates accordingly and gives you spoken directions. Tap the **Speaker** button for options to turn off spoken directions (mute) or to hear alerts only

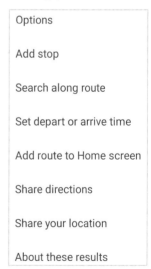

Tap on the **Menu** button on the top toolbar when viewing a location on a map, to access options such as adding the route to the Home screen and sharing your location.

Options
Add stop
Search along route
Set depart or arrive time
Add route to Home screen
Share directions
Share your location
About these results

113

Notes and Memos

Taking notes on an Android phone is an excellent way to keep up-to-date with a range of tasks, from shopping lists to reminders for packing for a trip. Several notes and memos apps can be downloaded from the Play Store, and most smartphone manufacturers include default notes and memos apps. The example here uses the **Keep Note** app, Google's own note-taking app. To use it:

Hot tip

Use these buttons at the top of the notes window to, from left to right: pin a note so that it always appears at the top of the Notes app's Home screen; add a reminder to a note; and archive a note (which removes it from the Notes app's Home screen):

1 Tap on the **Keep Note** app

2 Tap on this button to create a new note

3 Enter a title and body text for your note. Use the toolbars at the bottom of the screen to format the text of the note and also add more content, such as stickers and images

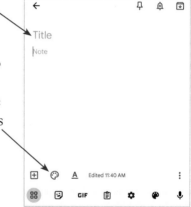

4 Enter the content for the note and tap on the back-pointing arrow to go back to the Home screen, which displays any other notes that have been created

114

Social Media

Social media has transformed the way in which we communicate, and there are numerous apps that can be used on an Android phone for social media. These can be downloaded from the Play Store, from within the **Social** category. Some of the most popular apps are:

Facebook

This is still one of the most widely used social media tools. To use Facebook you have to first register, which is free. You can then link up with your friends and share a variety of content, by searching for them and inviting them to join your network with a Friend Request.

Facebook

X (formerly Twitter)

X is a microblogging site where users post short messages (tweets). Once you have joined X, which is free, you can follow other users to see what they are saying and have people follow you too.

X

Snapchat

Snapchat is a messaging service that allows users to send photos and videos to their Snapchat friends or groups of people. Once these are accessed, they remain visible for a few seconds and are then deleted. Text and graphics can be added to items when they are sent – one of the most frequent uses is for sending self-portraits ("selfies" – see page 154).

Snapchat

Pinterest

This is an online pinboard where you can bookmark and "pin" items of interest and upload your own content for other people to pin.

Pinterest

Instagram

This is a popular photo- and video-sharing site. Followers can be added by users and they can then comment and "like" photos. Security settings should be checked to ensure that only the people you want are able to view your content (as with all social media sites).

Instagram

Don't forget

YouTube is one of the great successes of the internet age. It is a video-sharing site, with millions of video clips covering every subject imaginable. It is now owned by Google, and there is a pre-installed YouTube app on most Android phones that can be accessed from the **All Apps** button.

YouTube

Health and Fitness

Monitoring health and fitness with digital devices is a growth industry, and there is a good range of health and fitness apps that can record exercise activity on your Android phone. One of these is the **Google Fit** app. To use this:

1 Tap on the **Fit** app

Fit

2 Tap on this button to enter health and fitness information or start a new activity

3 Select an option from the menu – e.g. **Add activity**. This can be used for entering data for an activity that you have already undertaken

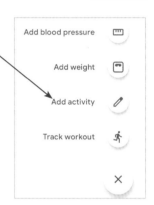

Add blood pressure

Add weight

Add activity

Track workout

✕

4 Select the type of activity that you want to record, and tap on the **Save** button

✕   Save ⋮

Add activity

Title   Add
Activity   Walking
Start   Today   3:56 PM
Duration   30 min

5 If **Track workout** is selected in Step 3, tap on the **Start** button to begin recording the workout activity. Tap on the **Pause** button to pause the workout recording

←
Activity type
🚶 Walking   ▾

▶
Start walking

Playing Games

Although computer games may seem like the preserve of the younger generation, this is definitely not the case. Not all computer games are of the shoot-em-up or racing variety, and the Play Store also contains puzzles and versions of popular board games. Some games to try are:

- **Chess**. Pit your wits against this Chess app. Various settings can be applied for each game, such as the level of difficulty.

- **Checkers**. Similar to the Chess app, but for Checkers (Draughts). Hints are also available to help develop your skills and knowledge.

- **Mahjong**. A version of the popular Chinese game, this is a matching game for single players, rather than playing with other people.

- **Scrabble**. An Android phone version of the best-selling word game that can be played with up to four people.

- **Solitaire**. An old favorite, the card game where you have to build sequences and remove all of the cards.

- **Sudoku**. The logic game where you have to fill different grids with numbers 1-9, without having any of the same number in a row or column.

- **Tetris**. One of the original computer games, where you have to piece together falling shapes to make lines.

- **Words With Friends**. Similar to Scrabble, an online word game played with other users.

Don't forget

As well as the games here, there is a full range of other types of games in the Play Store, which can be accessed from the **Games** category. They can also be accessed from the **Play Games** app.

Play Ga...

Around the Play Store

Although the pre-installed apps provide a lot of useful functionality and are a good starting point, the Play Store is where you can really start to take advantage of the wide range of apps that are available. These can be used for entertainment, communication, productivity, and much more.

To access the Play Store and find apps:

New apps are added to the Play Store on a regular basis (and existing ones are updated), so the Homepage will change appearance regularly.

1 Tap on the **Play Store** app

Play Store

2 Suggested items are shown on the Play Store Homepage, under the **For you** tab

The Play Store app opens at the screen that was last accessed when the app was previously used – i.e. the **Apps** section, if this is what was last used. By default, the Play Store opens at the **Games** section – see page 120.

page 120.

App prices are shown in the local currency.

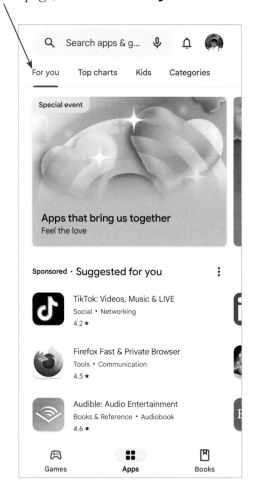

118

3 Swipe up and down or left and right to see the full range of recommendations for all types of content in the Play Store. Tap on an item to view further details about it

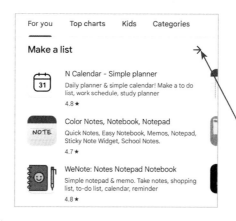

Tap on this button from a section on the Homepage to view additional items.

4 Use these buttons on the bottom toolbar to find relevant content: **Games**, **Apps**, and **Books**

5 Tap on the **Account** button to access the Play Store menu

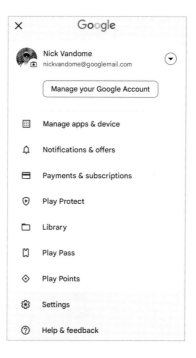

Finding Apps

Searching by category

When you have accessed the Play Store, you can then look for content in a variety of ways.

There may be different apps available in the Play Store, depending on your geographical location.

1 Featured and recommended items are displayed on the Homepage (by default, this opens on the **Games** section). Swipe up and down and left and right to view the full range, and tap on an item to view more details

2 Tap on the **Apps** button on the bottom toolbar to view the available range of apps. Swipe left and right on the top bar to view apps according to **For you**, **Top charts**, **Kids**, and **Categories**

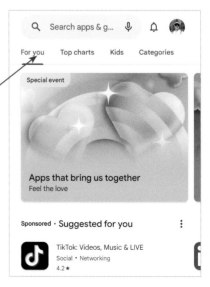

3 Tap on the **Categories** tab in Step 2 on the previous page, and tap on a category to view apps according to the relevant headings

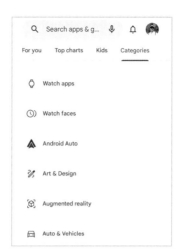

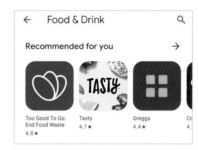

4 Search for apps within a category in the same way as for searching over a whole range of apps, as in Step 2 on the previous page

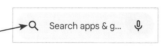

Using the Search box

1 Tap in the Search box on any page to conduct a search with keywords

2 Enter the name of an item for which you want to search

3 Tap on one of the suggested results, or tap on this button on the keyboard to conduct another search

As you type in the Search box, the suggested items will change, depending on the keyword(s) used.

Downloading Apps

Once you have found an app in the Play Store that you want to use, you can download it to your phone.

Hot tip

If you have a phone with 3G/4G/5G cellular capability, try downloading apps over Wi-Fi to avoid using too much of your data allowance.

Don't forget

If an app has a price button on it, you will need to add credit/debit card details to your Google Account. This can be done when the account is set up or from the Play Store menu (**Payment methods**).

Hot tip

Under **Settings** > **Apps**, select apps to apply settings for their notifications in the Notifications panel.

1 Access the app you want to use. There will be details about the app and reviews from other users if you scroll down the page

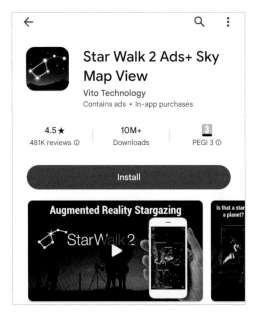

2 Tap on the **Install** button, and the app will start downloading

Install

3 Tap on the **Open** button to open the app once it has finished downloading and installing

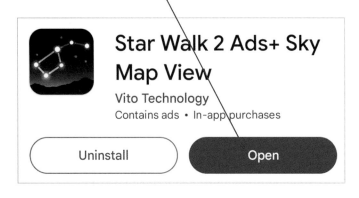

4 Some apps will ask to use your location, to improve their functionality. Select one of the options, as required, for giving permission for this

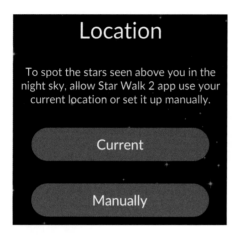

5 Tap on one of the options to give access to your location, or not

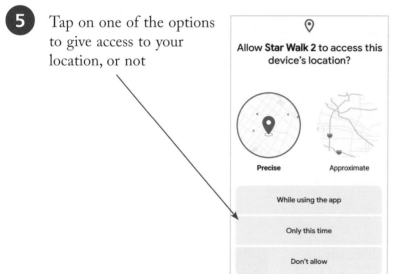

If an app has access to your device's location, it creates more location-specific content. If you deny an app permissions, it may not work as effectively.

6 Newly downloaded apps usually appear on the next available **All Apps** screen where there is a space. From here, the app can be opened and also moved to another location. A shortcut on your Home screen is sometimes also created

Uninstalling Apps

The pre-installed apps on an Android phone cannot be deleted easily (although they can be turned off), but ones that have been downloaded from the Play Store can be uninstalled. You may want to do this if you do not use a certain app any more or you feel the number of apps on your phone is becoming too great. To uninstall a downloaded app:

1 Access the **All Apps** section, or the Home screen, then press on an app and tap on the **App info** button

If apps have been uninstalled from the phone, they can be reinstalled from the Play Store app by tapping on your **Account** icon. Tap on the **Manage apps & device** option and tap on the **Manage** tab to view all of the apps that have previously been downloaded.

2 Tap on the **Uninstall** button to uninstall the app

Alternatively, press and hold on an app, drag it to the top of the screen and move it over the **Uninstall** button to uninstall the app.

Turning off pre-installed apps

Pre-installed apps cannot be uninstalled easily, but they can be turned off so that they cannot be used. This is done in a similar way to uninstalling apps.

1 Press and hold on the app to be turned off and tap on the **i** icon

Beware

2 Tap on the **Disable** button to continue and the **Disable app** option in the warning window

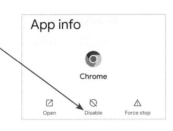

App info

Chrome

Open   Disable   Force stop

If you disable this app, Android and other apps may no longer function as intended. Keep in mind, you can't delete this app since it came pre-installed on your device. By disabling, you turn this app off and hide it on your device

Cancel   Disable app

Phone manufacturers can add their own apps to Android phones, and, in some cases, it is not possible to either uninstall or turn off these apps.

125

3 To turn the app back on, access **Settings** > **Apps** and tap on the disabled app

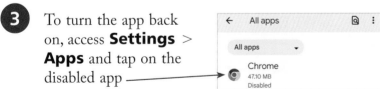

← All apps

All apps ▾

Chrome
47.10 MB
Disabled

4 Tap on the **Enable** button to turn the app back on

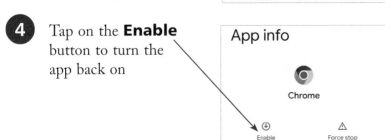

App info

Chrome

Enable   Force stop

Updating Apps

The world of apps is a dynamic and fast-moving one, and new apps are being created and added to the Play Store on a daily basis. Existing apps are also updated, to improve their performance and functionality. These can be added to your phone either automatically or manually.

Updating apps automatically

Apps are also updated to improve security features and include any fixes to improve the performance of the app.

1 Access the Play Store. Tap on the **Account** button and then the **Settings** button

Some app updates will require your confirmation before updating, even if you have chosen to auto-update apps.

2 Tap on the **Network preferences** option and tap on the **Auto-update apps** option

Network preferences
Data usage for downloads, auto-updates ⌄

Auto-update apps
Auto-update apps over Wi-Fi only

3 Tap on the **Over Wi-Fi only** radio button so that it contains a colored dot. Available updates will be installed automatically when the phone is connected to Wi-Fi

Auto-update apps

○ Over any network
Data charges may apply

◉ Over Wi-Fi only

○ Don't auto-update apps

Cancel   OK

Updating apps manually

Apps can also be updated manually.

1 Ensure **Don't auto-update apps** is selected in Step 3 on the previous page

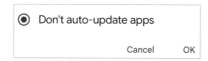

2 Access the Play Store. Tap on the **Account** button and then the **Manage apps & device** option

3 Tap on the **Overview** tab and on the **Update all** option to apply all available updates. Tap on the **See details** option to view information about the updates and update them individually

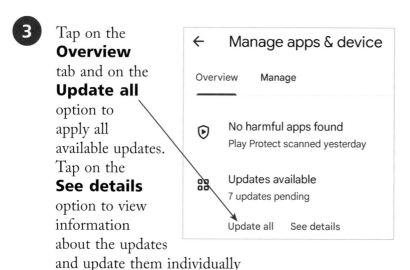

Beware

If apps are set to be updated manually, check regularly in the Play Store to see if there are any updates that you want to install for your apps.

App Information

For both pre-installed apps and those downloaded from the Play Store, it is possible to view details about them and also see the permissions that they are using to access certain functions. To view information about your apps:

Don't forget

Tap on the **Notifications** button in the **App info** window in Step 3 to specify how notifications are handled for the app. Drag the notifications button **On** to enable notifications to be displayed for the app.

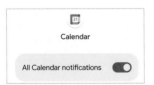

1 Open the **Settings** app and tap on the **Apps > See all [ ] apps** option

⠿ Apps
Assistant, recent apps, default apps

> See all 81 apps

2 Tap on an app to select it and view its details

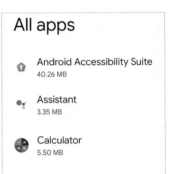

All apps

☂ Android Accessibility Suite
40.26 MB

• Assistant
3.35 MB

Calculator
5.50 MB

🗓 Calendar
48.92 MB

3 Tap on the **Force stop** button on the bottom toolbar to close a running app

4 Tap on the **Mobile data & Wi-Fi** option to view details about the size of the app and the amount of data it has stored

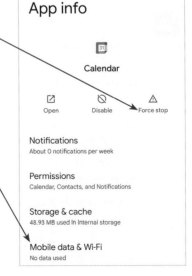

App info

🗓
Calendar

↗ Open   ⊘ Disable   ⚠ Force stop

Notifications
About 0 notifications per week

Permissions
Calendar, Contacts, and Notifications

Storage & cache
48.93 MB used in internal storage

Mobile data & Wi-Fi
No data used

8 Being Entertained

This chapter shows how to use your phone with music, movies, and for reading books.

130   Music on Android

134   Media Player

135   Google TV

138   Obtaining Ebooks

140   Around an Ebook

Music on Android

Accessing and playing music on smartphones with Android 13 is done through the **YT Music** app. This provides access to Google's huge catalog of music, much of which can be played for free on your Android smartphone. To use the **YT Music** app:

1 Tap on the **YT Music** app

130

2 Select five of your favorite artists from the first window. This will help the **YT Music** app tailor future suggestions and recommendations to your tastes

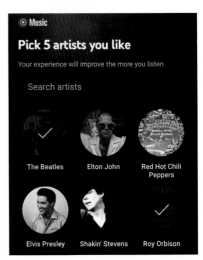

3 The **YT Music** app opens at the Homepage, which can also be accessed from the **Home** button on the bottom toolbar. Swipe along the top toolbar and tap on the categories to view their content

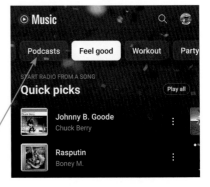

Home

...cont'd

4 Swipe down the Homepage to view the rest of its content and also access radio stations based on song selections

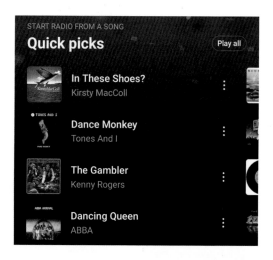

Tap on the **Search** icon at the top of the **YT Music** app to search for artists and tracks. Artists are listed with tracks, albums, playlists, and artists with whom they have collaborated.

5 Tap on the **Explore** button on the bottom toolbar to view the latest available music and suggested items

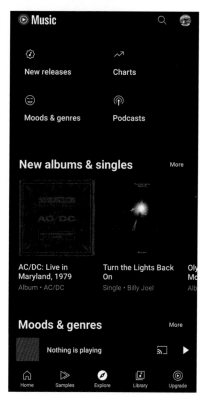

...cont'd

6 Tap on the **Library** button on the bottom toolbar and enter the name of an artist or band in the Search box at the top of the screen

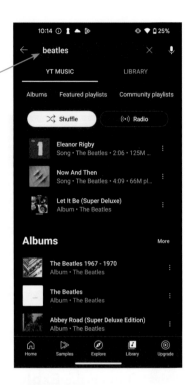

Tap on the **Upgrade** button on the bottom toolbar in Step 6 to upgrade to the **Music Premium** service, which is advert-free, provides a greater range of music, and allows you to download music so that you can listen to it when you are offline and not connected to the internet.

7 Tap on one of the search results to view the corresponding albums and tracks. Tap on the **Play** button to play a whole album, or tap on individual tracks to play them

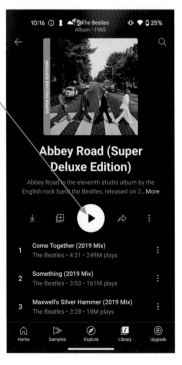

8 When a track is tapped on, it opens in its own music window, with music controls for the track. Tap here to minimize the music window so that you can continue exploring the **YT Music** app while the track is playing

Hot tip

Tap on the **Menu** button in the top right-hand corner of the window in Step 8 to access options for the current item being played.

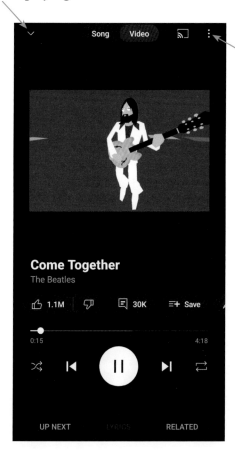

9 Use the music controls to, from left to right: shuffle tracks; go to the start of a track; pause or play a track; go to the end of a track; and repeat a track

The Media Player has been updated with Android 13.

If no method of Lock screen has been selected, the Media Player will not be available with any compatible apps.

Media Player

When playing music with the **YT Music** app or listening to podcasts with the **Podcasts** app, content is played within the app when you access it and the phone is unlocked. However, when the phone is locked, the content can still be listened to (in some instances; see below), via the Android Media Player on the Lock screen. To do this:

1 Open content in a compatible app – e.g. the **Podcasts** app. The content will play in its own app

2 Lock the screen for the phone by pressing the **On/Off** button once

3 Provided the phone has a method of Lock screen selected (PIN, password, pattern, etc.), the content will be displayed in the Media Player. This includes related artwork and an animated playback bar at the bottom of the screen

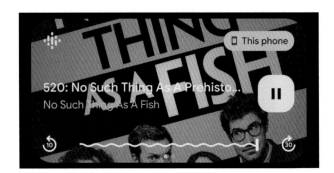

Podcasts usually play audio content, but some of them can include video too.

Content from the YT Music app also uses the Media Player in this way, but only if you subscribe to the Premium service; if not, the music will stop playing when the phone is locked. This prompt appears in the YT Music app when the phone is next unlocked:

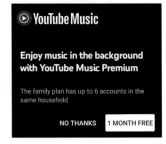

Google TV

The **Google TV** app is a way of watching movies and TV shows on your Android smartphone. It offers a significant range of content, including from different providers such as Disney+ and Amazon Prime. Content is streamed to your Android smartphone by default, which means it is played on your device without being downloaded onto it. To use the **Google TV** app:

1 Tap on the **Google TV** app

2 The **Google TV** app opens at the **For you** screen, which consists of recommended movies and TV shows

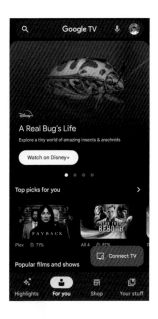

The content displayed on the **For you** screen changes regularly as new content is added.

135

3 Swipe down the screen to view the full range of available content

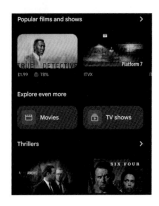

...cont'd

4 Tap on the **Movies** button in Step 3 on page 135 to view a range of available movies

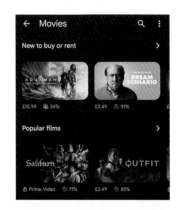

Don't forget

Movies and TV shows are displayed according to the geographic region in which the Android phone is being used.

5 Tap on the **TV shows** button in Step 3 on page 135 to view a range of available TV shows

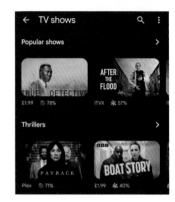

6 Tap on the **Shop** button on the bottom toolbar to view items that you can buy from Google TV

...cont'd

7 Tap on the arrow next to a category to view its full range of content

8 Swipe down the screen to view the full range of content that is on offer. Tap on an item to view its details

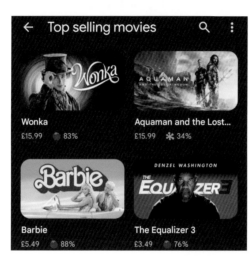

9 Tap on the **Connect TV** button on any screen and tap on the **Allow** button

to allow the app to discover compatible devices for playing content from Google TV – i.e. a smart TV

Beware

Rented items will be removed once the rental period expires.

Obtaining Ebooks

Due to their size and portability, Android phones are often used for reading ebooks. There is a wide range that can be downloaded using the Play Books app. To do this:

1   Tap on the **Play Books** app

2   Tap on the **Library** button on the bottom toolbar to view your titles. Tap on a cover to open a specific title

3   Tap on the **Shop** button on the bottom toolbar

4   Ebooks can be browsed for and downloaded in a similar way as for other Play Store content. Tap on these buttons to view the available categories

5   Tap on a title to view details about it

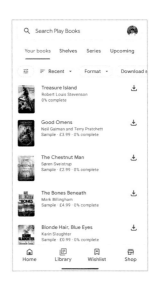

...cont'd

6 When you find an ebook you want to read, tap on the **Free sample** button (if there is one) or the **Buy** button (with the price)

7 When any ebook from the Play Books app has been downloaded to your phone, it is available within your Play Books Library

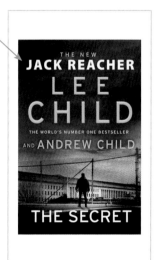

8 Simply select it to open it, and tap in the middle of the page to access the reading controls

Hot tip

The **Amazon Kindle** app can be downloaded from the Play Store for reading ebooks. If you already have a Kindle account, your ebooks will be available through the **Kindle** app on your phone.

Around an Ebook

Once you have downloaded ebooks to your phone, you can start reading them. Due to their format, there is a certain amount of electronic functionality that is not available in a hard copy version. To find your way around an ebook:

Don't forget

You can also move to the next or previous page of an ebook by tapping at the right-hand or left-hand edge of a page.

1 Swipe left and right on a page to move backward or forward by one page

2 Tap in the middle of a page to access the reading controls toolbars at the top and bottom of the screen

Search inside   Font size and formatting

←   Q   Aa   ⋮ — Settings menu

Return to library   Notes (Table of Contents)

≣⋮   ● ————————————— 2 / 241

3 Drag this button to move through the ebook

4 Tap on this button to access the ebook's Table of Contents, bookmarks, and notes

5 Tap on the **Menu** button to access the specific settings for the title you are reading

6 Tap on this button to select text options, including font size and line height

Aa

7 Tap in the top right-hand corner of a page to add a bookmark. A colored bookmark icon appears. Tap again to remove it. Tap on the button in Step 4 to view all bookmarks

eet between
il. His hand

9 Getting Things Done

This chapter introduces a range of apps for productivity tasks and storing documents.

142 Google Productivity Apps

143 Google Drive

146 Google Docs

150 Google Sheets

152 Google Slides

Google Productivity Apps

Google has created and used numerous apps and services over the years, some being more successful than others. One group that has flourished is the productivity apps, which contain Google Docs (word processing), Google Sheets (spreadsheets), Google Slides (presentations), and the online storage service, Google Drive (which can also be used as an app). These apps can be used individually on an Android phone and they can also be accessed from any online computer, using your Google Account sign-in details at **docs.google.com**, where all of the apps can be accessed.

Content that is created in the Google productivity apps is automatically saved when you are working with one of the apps, and it is also available in the Google Drive online storage app. It can also be accessed from an online computer if you want to continue working on it there.

The app versions of the Google productivity options are the default ones that are selected on an Android phone, even if the options are accessed through a web browser.

The Google Docs website can also be accessed from your own Google Account, where you can sign in at **myaccount. google.com**

1 Create a new document in one of the Google productivity apps on your phone

2 Access the same app on the Google Docs website, as above, to view the newly created document, and edit it as required

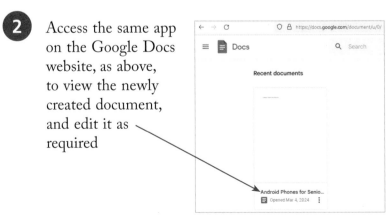

Google Drive

Google Drive is a cloud storage service, which means that its content is stored on Google's own computers, known as servers. Therefore, once something is saved to Google Drive you know it is safely stored, even if something goes badly wrong with your phone. Google Drive is accessed with your Google Account details, either through the website at **drive.google.com** or via the Google Drive app, which can be downloaded to your phone from the Play Store, if it is not already there. Google Drive works seamlessly with the Google productivity apps, so when you create anything in Docs, Sheets, or Slides, it is automatically saved in Google Drive. To start using Google Drive:

If a document is created in a productivity app (either in the app or through a web browser), it will also be available in your Google Drive app.

1. Tap on the **Drive** app on your phone, or download it from the Play Store

2. Tap on the **Home** button on the bottom toolbar to view options for uploading content to the Drive app

3. Tap on the **Files** button on the bottom toolbar to view content that has been added to the Drive app from other apps on your phone

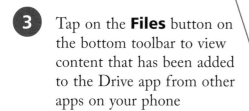

The contents of your Google Drive can also be accessed online, with your Google Account details, at drive.google.com

...cont'd

4 Tap on an item in the **Drive** app's **Files** section to view it at full size

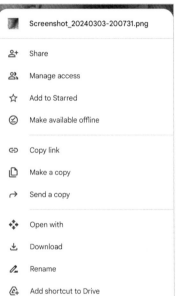

5 Tap on the **Menu** button in the top right-hand corner to view menu options for the item

Hot tip

Tap on the **Rename** option in Step 6 to rename a file or document in Google Drive.

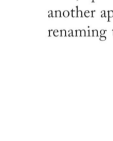
Rename

6 A range of options are available for the selected item, such as sharing it with people, copying the item, opening it with another app, and renaming the item

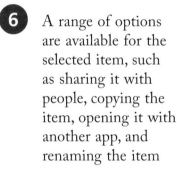

Don't forget

When you share an item from your Google Drive, the recipient is sent a link from which they can access the item; they are not sent the item itself.

7 Tap on the **Share** button in Step 6 to enable other people to view the item in your Google Drive. Enter an email address for the recipient and tap on the **Send** button

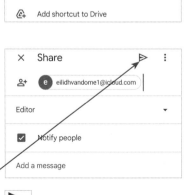

Adding content to Google Drive
To add new content within the Drive app:

1 Tap on the
+ New button
from any of the
options on the
bottom toolbar

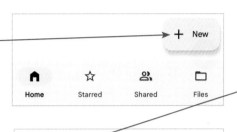

Tap on the **Folder**
option in Step 2 to
create a new folder
in your Google Drive,
which can be used to
organize items within
the Drive app.

2 Select options
for creating new
content, including
new documents in
the Google Docs,
Google Sheets,
and Google Slides
apps. These will appear in the **Files** section of the
Drive app

Adding content from other apps
To add content to Google Drive from other apps:

1 Select items in the
required app and
tap on this icon
to share the selected
items

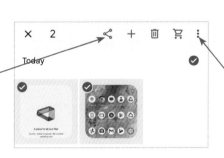

When adding images
to Google Drive from
the **Photos** app,
tap on the **Menu**
button and tap on the
Select option. Tap on
individual photos to
select them.

Select

2 Tap on the **Drive** option to share
the selected items to your Google
Drive

Share to Apps

Drive

145

Google Docs

Google Docs is the most popular of the Google productivity apps. It is a versatile word processor that can create attractively formatted documents and even save them into the Word file format, if required. To start with Google Docs:

1 If the app is not already on your phone, navigate to it in the Play Store and tap on the **Install** button

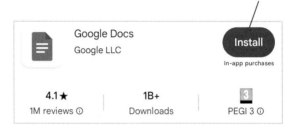

Google Docs
Google LLC
Install
In-app purchases

4.1 ★   1B+   **3**
1M reviews ①   Downloads   PEGI 3 ①

2 Tap on the **Docs** app on the Home screen to open Google Docs, which opens at its Home screen

Docs

3 Tap on this button to view files in list view

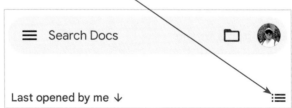

≡ Search Docs   📁   👤

Last opened by me ↓   ☰

4 Tap on this button to view files in grid view

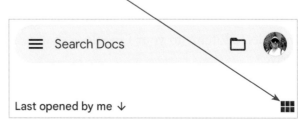

≡ Search Docs   📁   👤

Last opened by me ↓   ▦

...cont'd

5 Tap on this button to create a new Google Docs document

6 Tap on the **Choose template** option to create a document based on one with a preformatted layout. Tap on the **New document** option to create a new blank document

The text in Docs templates can all be overwritten when document is created. However, the text formatting will be retained, provided that you only select and overwrite sections that have their own formatting applied, rather than selecting everything in the document.

7 For the template option in Step 6, swipe up and down the page to view the various categories and the templates within them. Tap on one of the options to use that as the basis for your new document

...cont'd

Double-tap (or press and hold) on a word to select it, with resizing handles around it. Drag the resizing handles to increase the text selection. For more details about selecting text, see Chapter 5, page 94.

Once text has been selected, formatting can be applied to the selected text. However, if no text is selected, any formatting options will be applied as you enter text. For instance, if you have selected bold and a text color of red, this is what will appear as you enter text, until the formatting options are changed.

8 A new, as yet untitled, document is created based on the template selected in Step 7 on page 147 or as a blank page. For a template, example text is inserted, which can be selected and overwritten. The keyboard is available for entering text and a selection of toolbars for formatting text

9 Use this toolbar, at the top of the screen, to, from left to right: return to the app's Home screen; undo the previous action; redo the previous action; format text and paragraphs; insert content, such as images; add comments; and access the document's menu

10 Use this toolbar, directly below the text area, to, from left to right: add bold, italics, underlining, text color, highlight color, indent text; or add lists

11 Use this toolbar, above the keyboard, to, from left to right: expand the toolbar, add stickers, add GIF images, paste items from the clipboard, access settings, add a theme, or add text via voice

Saving and renaming documents

The Google productivity apps automatically save content as it is created. This content can then be confirmed and the document given a unique name. To do this:

1 When creating a document, tap on the checkmark (tick) to confirm the current text

If you do not tap on the checkmark (tick) in Step 1, any new text or changes to the document will still be saved, and this is how the document will appear when it is reopened.

2 At this point, the document is untitled. Tap on the back-pointing arrow to return to the Home screen

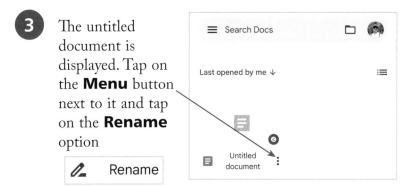

3 The untitled document is displayed. Tap on the **Menu** button next to it and tap on the **Rename** option

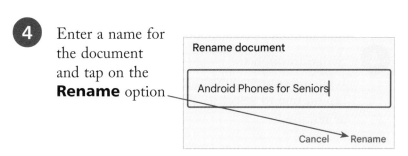

The process for saving and renaming documents is the same for Google Docs, Google Sheets, and Google Slides.

4 Enter a name for the document and tap on the **Rename** option

Rename document

Android Phones for Seniors

Cancel   Rename

149

Google Sheets

Google Sheets can be used to create spreadsheets, either just containing plain data or with formulas applied to make various calculations. To start using Google Sheets:

Don't forget

Spreadsheets can be used to compile straightforward lists, but they can also be used to perform complicated calculations using a range of formulas and commands. For an excellent introduction, and more, about using spreadsheets, see **Microsoft Excel in easy steps** in this series (Excel is the Microsoft spreadsheet app, but its operation is very similar to Google Sheets).

1 If Google Sheets is not already on your phone, download it from the Play Store in the same way as for Google Docs on page 146. Tap on the **Sheets** app on the Home screen to open Google Sheets, which opens at its Home screen

2 The Home screen includes any spreadsheets that you have already created or that have been shared with you. Tap on this button at the bottom of the screen to create a new spreadsheet

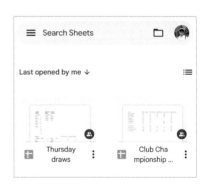

3 Select to create a spreadsheet from a template or a new blank spreadsheet, as with a Docs document

4 Swipe through the template options and tap on one to select it, as required

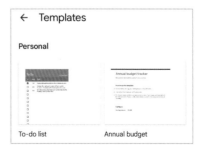

5 For a blank spreadsheet, there is no content in any of the cells. Tap on a cell to make it the active one and to display the toolbars

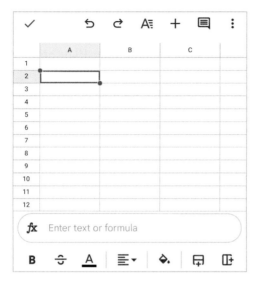

6 Use this toolbar at the top of the screen to, from left to right: return to the app's Home screen; undo the previous action; redo the previous action; format text and paragraphs; insert content, such as images; add comments; and access the document's menu

7 Use this toolbar below the spreadsheet's cells to enter text or formulas for the spreadsheets (see the Beware tip). From left to right: add bold, strikethrough, or text color to cell content; indent cell content; add cell color; add rows; and add columns

Hot tip

At the bottom of the screen of a new spreadsheet is a label for the title of the spreadsheet – e.g. **Sheet1**. Tap on this and tap on the **Rename** option to rename the sheet. This does not rename the overall spreadsheet document, though. Tap on the **+** button to add a new sheet within the spreadsheet.

Beware

Tap on the **fx** button in a text/formula box to access preset function commands, which require some knowledge of spreadsheet formulas. Tap in the text/formula box to access a toolbar below the box for a range of formulas that can be applied to calculations, such as = (equals) for calculating the total of a range of numbers.

Google Slides

Google Slides can be used to create presentations using a single slide or multiple slides, which can be used with transitions between each slide. To start using Google Slides:

Don't forget

Google Slides is similar to the widely used Microsoft PowerPoint. The toolbars at the top and bottom of the screen in Step 3 can be used to format content within a slide, add more slides, and control the overall operation of a slideshow.

1 If Google Slides is not already on your phone, download it from the Play Store in the same way as for Google Docs on page 146. Tap on the **Slides** app on the Home screen to open Google Slides, which opens at its Home screen

2 Access the option for creating a new presentation, as for Docs and Sheets

3 For a new presentation based on a template, the design is already created for the presentation and new text can overwrite the example text. Tap on this button at the top of the screen to return to the **Slides** Home screen

4 All presentations are displayed on the Home screen. Tap on one to edit it

10 Keeping in the Picture

This chapter shows how to make the most of the high-quality cameras that come with most Android phones.

154 Using Cameras

156 Adding Photos

158 Viewing Photos

161 Adding Albums

162 Editing Photos

164 Sharing Photos

Use the front-facing camera – i.e. the one on the phone's screen – to take "selfies," which are self-portraits that can also include other people.

Don't forget

The most recently captured photo is displayed on the bottom toolbar. Tap on it to open it in the **Photos** app.

Don't forget

Tap on the **Video** option in Step 2 to record a video rather than take a photo.

Using Cameras

Most Android phones have their own built-in cameras, which can be used to capture photos directly onto the device. The quality of these varies between makes of phone. Some are good-quality cameras intended to be used for taking photos in a range of conditions; others are mainly for use as a webcam for video calls or for "selfies" (these are front-facing cameras). To use an Android camera phone:

1. Tap on the **Camera** app

2. The **Camera** app displays the current scene, and control buttons are displayed at the side (landscape view) or at the bottom (portrait view)

3. Press on the screen to focus the current scene, and tap on this button to take a photo

4. Tap on this button to switch between the front- and rear-facing cameras

5. Swipe along the bottom of the screen to select different shooting options

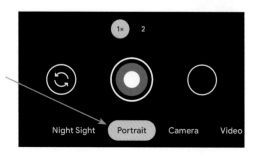

6 Further controls are available at the top of the screen

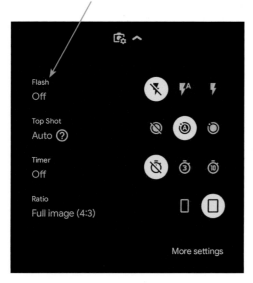

By default, photos captured with the Camera app are displayed in the **Photos** or **Gallery** apps.

7 Tap on the **More settings** button to view the full range of settings for the camera

8 Tap on one of the items to activate or deactivate it – e.g. saving the location of photos when they are captured (**Location** must be enabled for the Camera app for **Save location** to work)

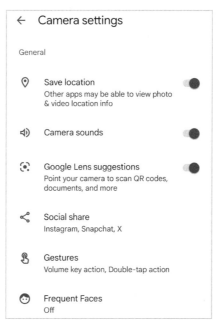

Different models of Android phones have their own cameras, which include specific settings and modes. However, the ones listed here will be similar across most Android cameras.

Adding Photos

Android phones are great for storing and, more importantly, displaying your photos. The screen size of most phones is ideal for looking at photos, and you can quickly transform it into your own mobile photo album. In addition, it is also possible to share all of your photos in a variety of ways.

Obtaining photos

In addition to capturing photos with your phone, you can obtain them in a number of ways:

- Transferring photos from your computer directly to your phone, via a USB cable (into the **Pictures** folder).

- Downloading and saving photos from an email, social media, a website, or from an internet messaging app.

- Transferring photos from another device via Bluetooth.

Once you have captured or transferred photos to your phone, you can then view, edit and share them using the **Photos** (or **Gallery**) app. Photos in the **Photos** app are stored in different albums that are created automatically when photos are taken, transferred, or downloaded from an email.

If you keep a lot of photos on your phone, this will start to take up storage space.

Personal videos can also be transferred in the same way as with photos. Copy them into the **Videos** folder of your computer. Videos can also be recorded with the **Video** button in the **Camera** app.

The **Photos** app is a Google app and is available in the Play Store if it is not pre-installed on a phone.

Downloading from email

Email is a good method of obtaining photos on your phone; other people can send their photos to you in this way, and you can also email your own photos from a computer, a tablet or another mobile device. To use photos from email:

 Open an email containing a photo and tap on this button to download it

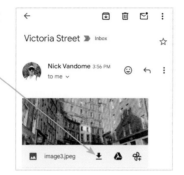

Once the **Download** folder has been created, all other photos downloaded from emails will be placed here.

157

2 The photo will be saved in the **Download** folder within the **Photos** app. The folder will be automatically created if it is not already there

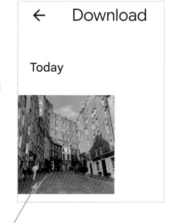

3 Tap on the photo to open the album, and tap on it again to view it at full size in the **Photos** app, where it can be edited, as required

Viewing Photos

Once you have obtained photos on your Android phone, you can start viewing, managing, and editing them.

1 Open the **Photos** app and tap on the **Library** button at the bottom of the screen to view the available options within it

The default albums in the **Photos** app are initially empty.

2 Tap on the **View all** option in the **Photos on device** section to view all of the photos on your Android phone

Tap on the **Photos** button at the bottom of the screen to view photos that have been taken with the phone.

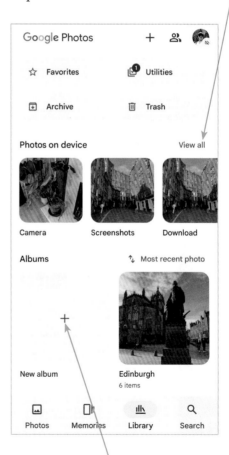

3 Tap here to create a new album for storing photos; see page 161 for details

Photos in the **Photos** app can be worked with and viewed in different ways.

1 Open the **Photos** app and tap on the **Photos** button on the bottom toolbar

2 Photos are displayed in date order, with the most recent at the top of the screen

Swipe up the page in Step 2 to view your photos in date order.

3 Tap on a photo to view it at full size

...cont'd

4 Press and hold on photos to select them

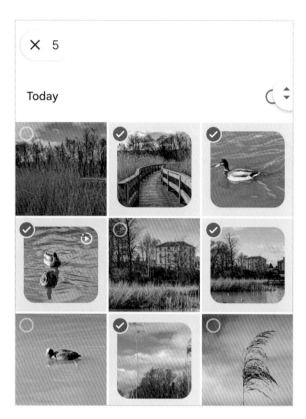

Hot tip

Items selected in Step 4 can be shared in a variety of ways by tapping on this button (see page 164 for details):

5 Use the toolbar below the images to apply actions to the selection. These include, from left to right: sharing the selection; adding the selection to an album, a movie, an animation or a collage; deleting the selected item(s); or ordering an online photo book with the selection

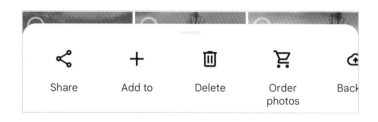

Adding Albums

In addition to the pre-inserted device albums, new ones can be added from the **Library** section of the **Photos** app. To do this:

1 Tap on the **Library** button

2 Tap on the **+** button under the **Albums** heading

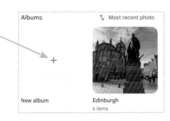

3 Give the album a name, then tap on the **+ Select photos** option

4 Tap on the photos to be included in the album, then tap on the **Add** button

5 The photos are added to the new album, which is included in the **Albums** section in the **Library**

Hot tip

Individual photos can be added to albums by viewing them at full size, tapping on the **Menu** button in the top right-hand corner of the screen, tapping on the **Add to album** option, and selecting the required album.

Editing Photos

Although the **Photos** app is more for viewing photos, it does have a few editing options so that you can tweak and enhance your images. To access and use these:

 Tap on a photo to view it. Tap on the **Edit** button on the bottom toolbar to access editing options

Hot tip

For more help with taking and editing photos on your phone, check out Smartphone Photography in easy steps and 100 Top Tips – Create Great Photos Using Your Smartphone at www.ineasysteps.com

 Tap on the **Enhance** button to access options for applying quick (one-tap) editing options to the photo

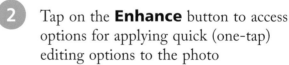

Beware

Add small editing changes at a time; otherwise, the effect may look too severe.

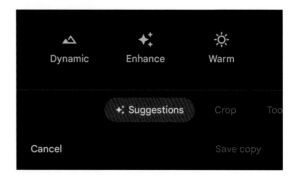

3 Swipe along the bottom toolbar and tap on the **Adjust** button to access a range of color-editing functions, including editing the brightness and color contrast of the photo

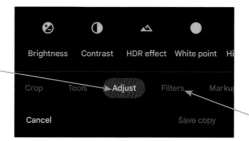

Tap on the **Filters** option in Step 3 to apply colored filters to the photo being edited. Tap on a filter thumbnail to apply it to the photo.

4 Tap on the **Adjust** options to expand them and access sliders for editing elements for the selection

5 To crop a photo, tap on the **Crop** button on the toolbar in Step 3 and drag the resizing handles to crop the photo

Most photos benefit from some cropping, to give the main subject more prominence.

6 Tap on this button to rotate the photo manually, clockwise or anti-clockwise

7 Tap on the **Save copy** button to save any editing changes that have been made

163

Social networking sites such as Facebook and X (formerly Twitter) are ideal for sharing photos. Their respective apps can be downloaded from the Play Store, in which case they will also appear as one of the sharing options in Step 2 opposite.

Beware

If you are sending photos by Bluetooth, the other device must be paired with your phone, have Bluetooth turned on, and accept the request to download photos when they are sent. When pairing two devices, a password will usually be created on the first device that then needs to be entered into the second device.

Sharing Photos

It can be great fun and very rewarding to share photos with friends and family. With an Android phone, this can be done in different ways.

1 Open a photo at full size and tap on the **Share** button

2 Select one of the sharing options. This will be dependent on the apps on your phone, but should include email, messaging, and online storage options such as **Google Drive**

Sharing with Bluetooth

To share with another device using Bluetooth:

1 Access a photo or make a selection of photos (as shown in Step 4 on page 160) then tap on the **Share** button and then the **Bluetooth** option, from the **More** button in Step 2 above

Bluetooth

2 If your Bluetooth is not on, turn it **On** in the **Settings** app

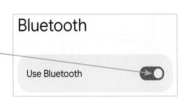

3 Select the device with which you want to share your photo(s). These will be sent wirelessly via Bluetooth

11 Online with Chrome

This chapter looks at browser options on Android and also viewing all of your favorite websites with the Chrome browser.

166 Android Web Browsers

167 Opening Pages

168 Bookmarking Pages

170 Links and Images

171 Using Tabs

172 Being Incognito

173 Browser Settings

Mobile versions of a website usually have **m.** before the rest of the website address – e.g. **m.mysite.com**

Android Web Browsers

Web browsing is an essential part of our digital world, and on Android phones this functionality can be provided by a variety of web browsers customized for this purpose. They can usually display websites in two ways:

- Optimized for viewing on mobile devices, which are versions that are designed specifically for viewing in this format.

- Full versions of websites (rather than the mobile versions), which are the same as those used on a desktop computer.

Different Android phones have different default browsers but they all have the same general functionality:

- Viewing web pages.

- Bookmarking pages.

- Tabbed browsing – i.e. using tabs to view more than one web page within the same browser window.

If you do not want to use the default browser that is provided with your phone, there is a range of browsers that can be downloaded, for free, from the Play Store.

Enter **browsers for android** into the **Play Store Search box** to view the available options.

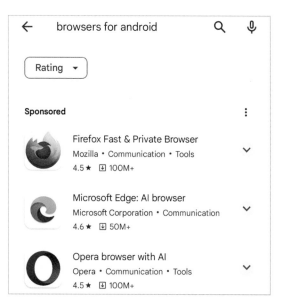

Opening Pages

Web pages can be opened on a phone in an almost identical way as on a desktop computer or laptop. Some Android web browsers display a list of top sites when you open a browser or create a new tab. (The examples on the following pages are for Google's **Chrome** browser, but other browsers operate in a similar way.)

Don't forget

The Chrome browser can be downloaded from the Play Store if it is not already on your phone. This is a Google product and integrates closely with other Google apps on your phone.

1 The **Search/Address** box can be used to search for keywords or phrases, or you can use it to find specific web pages and sites. Enter text into the **Search/Address** box. If a web address is displayed, tap on it to go directly to that website

2 Next, tap on the Search icon to search for the item on the web. Tap on an item in the search results list to view it

Hot tip

Swipe outward with your thumb and forefinger on a web page to zoom in on it; pinch inward to zoom back out. You can double-tap with one finger to zoom in and out too, but this zooms in to a lesser degree than swiping.

3 For a web address – e.g. one that ends in .com – the web page will be opened; if you have just entered a keyword in the **Search/Address** box, then the results page will be opened for that keyword. Tap one of the links as required

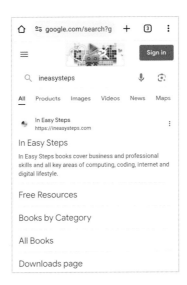

Bookmarking Pages

Your favorite web pages can be bookmarked so that you can find them quickly. To do this:

1 Open a page that you want to bookmark and tap on the **Menu** button at the top of the window

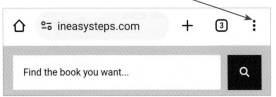

2 Tap on this icon to bookmark the page

Hot tip

If bookmarks are saved into the **Mobile bookmarks** folder, they will also be available on other mobile devices when you are signed in to your Google Account.

168

3 Tap on the **Bookmark saved in** option

4 By default, the bookmark is placed into the Mobile bookmarks folder. Tap on the **Mobile bookmarks** option to edit its details

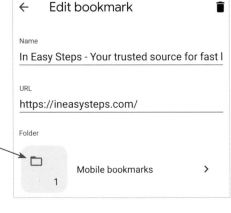

Don't forget

Tap the **Delete** icon in Step 4 to remove the bookmark.

5 Tap on a folder to select it, or tap on the **New folder** button to create a new folder to use

Mobile bookmarks

6 Give the folder a name, and tap on the **Add** button to create the folder. Then, tap on the back arrow button to save and return to the previous screen

Create new folder

Title

Computing

Cancel   Add

←

Don't forget

The **Menu** button in Step 1 can also be used to open a new tab. See page 171 for more details about using tabs.

Viewing bookmarks

To view pages that have been bookmarked:

1 To view bookmarks, tap on the **Menu** button and tap on the **Bookmarks** option

★ Bookmarks

Hot tip

Tap on the **Menu** button next to a bookmarked web page and tap on the **Move to...** option, to move the bookmark to a different location – e.g. another folder.

2 If folders have been created, tap on one to view its contents

3 Tap on a bookmarked page to open the page in the **Chrome** browser

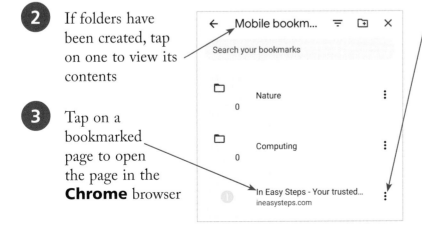

← Mobile bookm... ☰ 🗀 ✕

Search your bookmarks

🗀   Nature
     0

🗀   Computing
     0

ℹ️   In Easy Steps - Your trusted...
     ineasysteps.com

Select

Edit

Move to...

Links and Images

Links and images are both essential items on websites; links provide the functionality for moving between pages and sites, while images provide the all-important graphical element. To work with these:

Tap on the **Share link** option in Step 1 to send a link to someone via options including email, text message or social media sites.

1 Tap and hold on a link to access its options (tap once on a link to go directly to the linked page). The options include opening the link in a new tab, opening it in a new tab that does not get recorded by the browser's history (**Open in Incognito tab**), copying the web address or link text so that it can be shared with someone or pasted into a document, and downloading the link so that it can be viewed offline

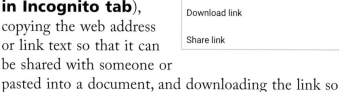

iPad for Seniors in easy steps, 13t...
ineasysteps.com/products-page/i...

Open in new tab in group

Open in new tab

Open in Incognito tab

Preview page

Copy link address

Download link

Share link

Google Lens is an app that can search for items based on images rather than a textual description or keywords. Google Lens can use images on the web, or those taken by the camera on your Android phone. It can be downloaded from the Play Store.

2 Tap and hold on an image to access its options. The options include viewing it on its own (**Open image in new tab**), downloading it, searching Google for the image, or sharing the image

iPad for Seniors in easy steps, 13th edition 9781787910065 front cover

Open image in new tab

Preview image

Copy image

Download image

Search image with Google Lens ᴺᵉʷ

Share image

Using Tabs

Tabs are a common feature on web browsers and allow you to open numerous pages within the same browser window. To do this on an Android phone, using Chrome:

1 Tap on this button in the top right-hand corner of the browser window to view current tabs

 Don't forget

The button in Step 1 displays the number of tabs currently open within the **Chrome** browser.

2 Tap on this button to add a new tab

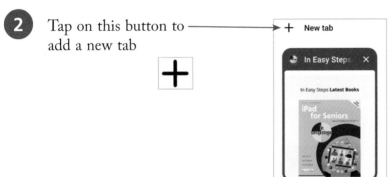

3 Open a new page from the **Search or type URL** box or any bookmarked pages that are displayed

Hot tip

If there are a lot of tabs open, swipe up and down in the tabs window in Step 4 to view them.

4 Tap on the tab button in Step 1 to view all tabs. Tap on a page to open it. Press and hold on the top of a page and drag it into a different position on the tabs screen

Being Incognito

If you do not want a record to be kept of the web pages that you have visited, most browsers have a function where you can view pages "in private" so that the details are not stored by the browser. In Chrome, this is performed with the **Incognito** function.

If the **Incognito** option is used, web pages will not be stored in the browser history or the search history.

1 Tap on the **Menu** button and tap on the **New Incognito tab** option

2 The Incognito page opens in a new tab, but any other open tabs are not visible (unless they are Incognito too). Open a web page in the same way as for a standard tab

If children are using your phone, you may not know what they are looking at on the web if they use the **Incognito** option.

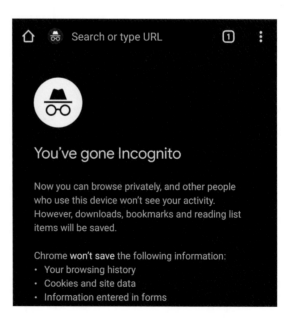

You've gone Incognito

Now you can browse privately, and other people who use this device won't see your activity. However, downloads, bookmarks and reading list items will be saved.

Chrome **won't save** the following information:
- Your browsing history
- Cookies and site data
- Information entered in forms

172

3 Incognito pages are denoted by this icon in the top left-hand corner of the browser

Browser Settings

Mobile browsers have the usual range of settings that can be accessed from the **Menu** button.

1 Tap on the **Menu** button and tap on the **Settings** option

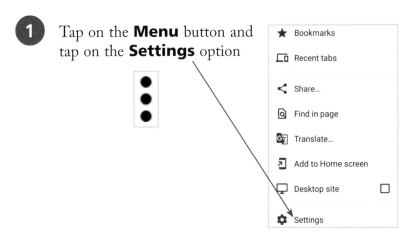

★ Bookmarks

⊡ Recent tabs

◁ Share...

▣ Find in page

G⊠ Translate...

⬈ Add to Home screen

⬚ Desktop site ☐

⚙ Settings

Some of the settings include:

- **Search engine**. This can be used to set a default search engine for the browser.

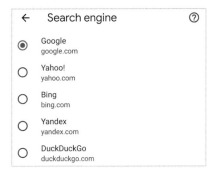

← Search engine ⑦

◉ Google
google.com

○ Yahoo!
yahoo.com

○ Bing
bing.com

○ Yandex
yandex.com

○ DuckDuckGo
duckduckgo.com

- **Password Manager**. Use this to make selections for how passwords are dealt with by the browser.

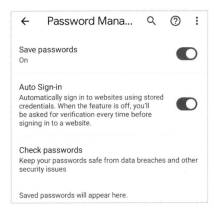

← Password Mana... 🔍 ⑦ ⋮

Save passwords
On ●

Auto Sign-in
Automatically sign in to websites using stored credentials. When the feature is off, you'll be asked for verification every time before signing in to a website. ●

Check passwords
Keep your passwords safe from data breaches and other security issues

Saved passwords will appear here.

Beware

If other people are going to be using your account on your phone, do not turn on the **Auto Sign-in** option for websites in the **Password Manager** section.

...cont'd

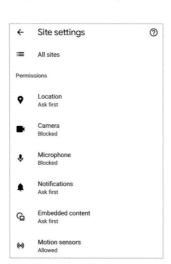

Don't forget

A cookie is a small piece of data that is stored by the browser, containing information about websites that have been visited.

- **Privacy and security**. Use this to specify how your browsing data is used.

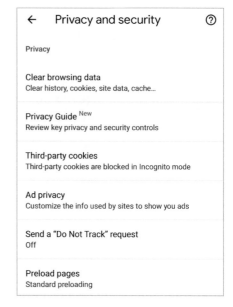

← Privacy and security   ⑦

Privacy

Clear browsing data
Clear history, cookies, site data, cache...

Privacy Guide ᴺᵉʷ
Review key privacy and security controls

Third-party cookies
Third-party cookies are blocked in Incognito mode

Ad privacy
Customize the info used by sites to show you ads

Send a "Do Not Track" request
Off

Preload pages
Standard preloading

- Under the **Advanced** heading, select options including **Accessibility**, to specify the text size for viewing web pages, and **Site settings**, where you can select options for the permissions that certain functions on your phone can be given.

Advanced

Homepage
On

Toolbar shortcut

Accessibility

Site settings

← Site settings   ⑦

☰   All sites

Permissions

📍   Location
    Ask first

🎥   Camera
    Blocked

🎤   Microphone
    Blocked

🔔   Notifications
    Ask first

  Embedded content
    Ask first

((•))   Motion sensors
    Allowed

12 Staying Secure

This chapter looks at security and privacy issues, your overall digital wellbeing, and parental controls.

176 Security Issues

177 About Antivirus Apps

178 Security and Privacy

182 Digital Wellbeing

184 Parental Controls

186 Locating Your Phone

Security Issues

Security is a significant issue for all forms of computing, and this is no different for Android phone users. Three main areas of concern are:

- **Getting viruses from apps**. Android apps can contain viruses like any other computer programs, but there are antivirus apps that can be used to try to detect viruses. Unlike programs on computers or laptops with file

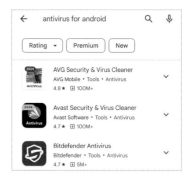

management systems, apps on a phone tend to be more self-contained and do not interact with the rest of the system. This means that if they do contain viruses, it is less likely that they will infect the whole phone.

- **Losing your phone or having it stolen**. If your phone is lost or stolen, you will want to try to get it back and also lock it remotely so that no one else can gain access to your data and content. The Android **Settings** app has an option for finding a lost phone (see page 186), and some antivirus apps also have this option.

- **Restricting access for children**. If you have young children or grandchildren who are using your phone, you will want to know what they are using it for. This is particularly important for the web, social media sites, video-sharing sites, and

messaging sites where there is the potential to interact with other people. There is also a range of parental control apps that can be downloaded from the Play Store. These can be used to limit access to certain types of apps or content.

About Antivirus Apps

Android phones are certainly not immune from viruses and malware, and the FBI's Internet Crime Complaint Center (IC3) has even published advice and information about malicious software aimed at Android users. Some general precautions that can be taken to protect your phone are:

- Use an antivirus app on your phone. There are several of these, and they can scan your phone for any existing viruses and also check new apps and email attachments for potential problems.

- Apps that are provided in the Play Store are checked for viruses before they are published, but if you are in any doubt about an app, research it online before you download it. If you do an online search for an app, any issues related to it should be available.

- Do not download any email attachments if you are not sure of their authenticity. If you do not know the person who has sent the email, then delete it.

Functionality of antivirus apps

There are several antivirus apps available in the Play Store. Search for "android antivirus apps" (or similar) to view the apps. Most security apps have a similar range of features:

- **Scanning** for viruses and malicious software (malware).

- **Online protection** against malicious software on websites.

- **Anti-theft protection**. This can be used to lock your phone, locate it through **Location Services**, wipe its contents if they are particularly sensitive, and instruct it to let out an alert sound.

For some of the functions of antivirus and security apps, a sign-in is required.

A lot of antivirus and security apps are free, but there is usually a Pro or Premium version that has to be paid for. It is worth downloading several of the free versions of antivirus apps to see how you like them and to try out the different functions that they have.

Some antivirus apps also have an option for backing up items such as your contacts, which can then be restored to your phone or another device if they are deleted or corrupted.

The security and privacy features have been enhanced and updated for phones using Android 13.

Swipe down the screen in Step 3 to view the full range of security and privacy options.

Security and Privacy

Privacy, and how your personal data is used, is of increasing importance in the digital world. With Android phones using Android 13, there are a number of privacy settings that can be applied to ensure that you have as much control as possible over your data. To use these:

1 Tap on the **Settings** app

Settings

2 Tap on the **Security & privacy** tab

Security & privacy
App security, device lock, permissions

3 Tap on the **Scan device** button to perform a virus scan on your device

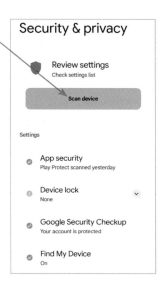

4 The results of the scan are displayed. Tap on the **Scan** button to perform another scan. Recently scanned apps are shown below the **Scan** button

...cont'd

Security Checkup
To perform a general security check on your phone:

1 Tap on the **Google Security Checkup** option in Step 3 on the previous page

Google Security Checkup
Your account is protected

2 **Security Checkup** items are displayed. A green icon indicates that no action is required; a blue icon indicates that action is required; an orange icon indicates that urgent action is required

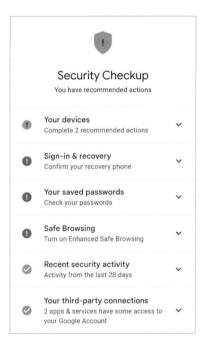

Security Checkup
You have recommended actions

Your devices
Complete 2 recommended actions

Sign-in & recovery
Confirm your recovery phone

Your saved passwords
Check your passwords

Safe Browsing
Turn on Enhanced Safe Browsing

Recent security activity
Activity from the last 28 days

Your third-party connections
2 apps & services have some access to
your Google Account

3 Tap on the **Your devices** option in Step 2 above to view recommended security actions for your phone

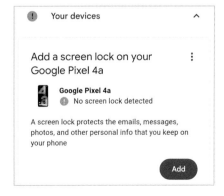

Your devices

Add a screen lock on your
Google Pixel 4a

Google Pixel 4a
No screen lock detected

A screen lock protects the emails, messages,
photos, and other personal info that you keep on
your phone

Add

Beware

If your phone does not have a screen lock, anyone could gain unauthorized access to it and view all of your personal information and content on the phone.

...cont'd

4 Tap on the **Sign-in & recovery** option in Step 2 on page 179 to set a phone number for help with signing in to your phone if you forget your sign-in details

5 Tap on the **Your saved passwords** option in Step 2 on page 179 to check your passwords and update them, if required

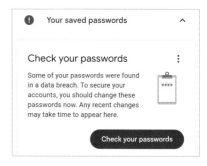

If **Enhanced Safe Browsing** is applied in Step 6, this will prevent a range of malicious content from being able to access your phone and also prevent inappropriate items from being viewed in the Chrome web browser.

6 Tap on the **Safe Browsing** option in Step 2 on page 179 to turn on **Enhanced Safe Browsing** in the Chrome web browser, to create a safer browsing environment

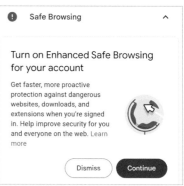

7 Tap on the **Recent security activity** option in Step 2 on page 179 to view any security activity in the last 28 days

...cont'd

Privacy

To view general privacy options on your phone:

1 Tap on the **Privacy** option further down the screen in Step 3 on page 178

2 Privacy items are displayed

3 Tap on the **Privacy dashboard** option in Step 2 above to view how apps have interacted with items on your phone, such as location services, the camera and the microphone

Beware

The greater the number of items that have permission to access apps on your phone, in Step 4, the greater the risk of security breaches. However, some apps require this type of permission to operate properly – e.g. the **Phone** app requires permission to use the device's microphone in order to make calls.

4 Tap on the **Permission manager** option in Step 2 above to access items and allow or prevent apps from interacting with them

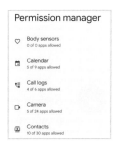

5 Tap on the **Privacy controls** option in Step 2 above to apply or prevent specific privacy options, such as showing or hiding passwords as you enter them

The digital wellbeing
features have been
enhanced and updated
for phones using
Android 13.

For the items in
Step 4: **Bedtime
mode** can be used to
silence items on your
phone and dim the
lighting on the screen,
to make it easier to fall
asleep (another option
is to turn off the
phone instead); **Focus
mode** can be used
to pause certain apps
and hide notifications
so that you can
focus on specific
tasks; **Manage
notifications** can
be used to specify
which apps can send
you notifications; and
Do Not Disturb
can be used to silence
notifications and calls,
except for people or
apps that you specify.

Digital Wellbeing

As we all spend more time on our digital devices, there is
an increasing awareness of the need to keep control of our
screen usage. With Android 13, this can be done with the
Digital Wellbeing & parental controls settings,
which allow you to track and limit your screen time and also
apply a range of wellbeing settings. To do this:

1 Tap on the **Settings** app

Settings

2 Tap on the **Digital
Wellbeing & parental
controls** option

Digital Wellbeing & parental
controls
Screen time, app timers, bedtime schedules

3 Details of your
current screen time usage
are displayed, including
apps that have been used

Digital Wellbeing &
parental controls

Your Digital Wellbeing tools

Other

Play Store

TODAY
28 minutes

Photos

Chrome

–
Unlocks ⓘ

6
Notifications

Ways to disconnect

4 Swipe down the screen
to view all of the Digital
Wellbeing options,
including **Bedtime
mode**, **Focus mode**,
Manage notifications,
and **Do Not Disturb**

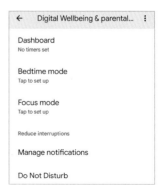

← Digital Wellbeing & parental...   ⋮

Dashboard
No timers set

Bedtime mode
Tap to set up

Focus mode
Tap to set up

Reduce interruptions

Manage notifications

Do Not Disturb

Screen time

To use the **Screen time** option to control your screen usage:

1 Tap on the **Screen time** circle in Step 3 on the previous page

2 Details about daily screen time are displayed in a graph at the top of the screen

3 Screen time for individual apps is shown further down the screen. Tap on an app to view its screen time details

Hot tip

Tap on the timer icon next to an item on the Dashboard screen to access the same app timer as in Step 5.

4 Tap on the **Daily** button to select options for how the app's screen time information is displayed

5 Tap on the **App timer** option to select a timer for the length of time that the app can be used

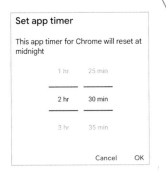

Hot tip

Tap on the **Screen time** option in Step 4 to select options for what is displayed on the screen.

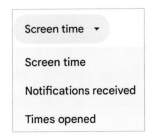

Parental Controls

If grandchildren or teens are going to have access to your Android phone, it is important to know exactly what type of content they are accessing and watching. To help with this, parental controls can be set up so that you can monitor their usage on your phone and restrict access to certain items. To start setting this up:

Beware

If you are setting parental controls for grandchildren, make sure that you tell them what you have done, and why, so that they fully understand why certain options may not be available.

1 Swipe to the bottom of the **Digital Wellbeing and parental controls** screen in Step 4 on page 182 and tap on the **Set up parental controls** option

> Families
>
> **Parental controls**
> Add content restrictions and set other limits to help your child balance their screen time
>
> Set up parental controls

2 Tap on the **Get started** button to start setting up parental controls

Set up parental controls

with Google's Family Link

- Supervise this phone remotely with the Family Link app for parents
- Keep an eye on screen time and set limits as needed
- Add restrictions to Google services, like app approvals or content filters on Google Play

Get started

3 If parental controls are to be set up on your own phone, tap on the **Parent** button

Who will be using this device?

Child or teen

Parent

4 Tap on the **Get Family Link** button to download the Family Link app, which is used to set up parental controls

Install Family Link

Use the Family Link app to remotely supervise your child's Android device

Get Family Link

Beware

Children or teens need their own Google Account on their phone in order to use the **Family Link** app for setting up parental controls on your phone.

5 Tap on the **Install** button to install the Family Link app, and tap on it on the Home screen to open it

← Google Play

Google Family Link
Google LLC

4.5 ★   100M+
2M reviews   Downloads   PEGI 3

Install

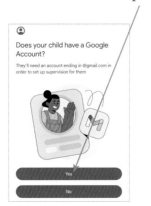

Family Link

6 As you are signed in on your Android phone with your own Google Account, tap on the **Continue as [ ]** button, and tap on the **Yes** button to continue setting up parental controls (see tips)

Welcome to Family Link

With Family Link you can see how your children spend their time on their devices and help manage their activity remotely

Google

Nick Vandome
nickvandome@googlemail.com

Continue as Nick

Don't forget

Certain steps have to be completed on the child's or teen's phone in order for parental controls to take effect.

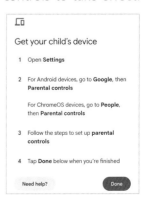

Get your child's device

1 Open **Settings**

2 For Android devices, go to **Google**, then **Parental controls**

   For ChromeOS devices, go to **People**, then **Parental controls**

3 Follow the steps to set up **parental controls**

4 Tap **Done** below when you're finished

Need help?   Done

Does your child have a Google Account?

They'll need an account ending in @gmail.com in order to set up supervision for them

Yes

No

Locating Your Phone

If you lose your phone or it is stolen, you can try to find its location via the **Find My Device** option.

A lost phone has to be turned on and **Location** enabled in **Settings** > **Location** for it to be located via the **Find My Device** feature.

Depending on the type of Android phone you are using, you may need to link it to an account belonging to your phone's manufacturer as part of the initial process for activating **Find My Device**.

Hot tip

The Google website can also be used to find a lost phone, using your Google Account. This can be set up via **Settings** > **Google** > **Find My Device**.

1. Access **Settings** > **Security & privacy** and tap on the **Find My Device** option

   Find My Device
   Off

2. Drag the **Use Find My Device** button **On**

3. Your phone can be tracked from the website of your Android manufacturer. Select options for the functionality of the **Find My Device** function, such as playing an alert sound, being able to remotely lock your phone if it is lost or stolen, and erasing the contents from the phone

Index

Symbols

3G networks	18
4G networks	18
5G networks	18

A

Accented letters.	.
See Keyboard: Accented letters	
Adding contacts from a call	70
Address book	109
All Apps	42, 46
Android	
Characteristics	8
Checking version	9
Overview	8
Updating	10
Version names	9
Viewing version	10
Android 13 features	14-15
Android apps	108-109
Antivirus apps	177
Apps	
Adding to the Home screen	46
Android apps	108-109
Closing	45
Downloading	122-123
Finding	120-121
Force stopping	128
Google apps	110-111
Information	128
In the Play Store	118-119
Moving	47
New	118
Uninstalling	124
Updating automatically	126
Updating manually	127
Using	26
Auto-rotate	40

B

Back button	45
Background	
Changing	52
Bluetooth	
Sharing photos	164
Books.	*See also* Ebooks
Obtaining	138-139
Buttons	
Navigation	45

C

Calls	
Accepting	78
End call	80
Making	76-77
Receiving	78-80
Rejecting	78
Rejecting with a text message	78
Speaker	79
Camera	154-155
Controls	155
For video calls	154
Using	154-155
Caps Lock	86
Cellular networks	18
Chrome browser 167. *See also* Websites	
Connecting to the internet	
With Wi-Fi	19
Contacts	
Adding	68
Editing	72-73
Managing	74-75
Saving from a call	70
Saving from texts	71
Searching for	77
Cookies	174

D

Digital Wellbeing	182-185
Bedtime mode	182
Do Not Disturb	182
Focus mode	182
Manage notifications	182
Docs.	See Google Docs
Drive.	See Google Drive

E

Ebooks	
Around	140
Reading controls	140
Table of Contents	140
Email 102-103.	See also Gmail
Adding an account	102-103
Attachment security	177
Setting up	102-103
Emojis	98-99
From the Suggestion strip	99
Recently used	98
Viewing categories	99

F

Facebook	115, 164
Favorites	48
Favorites Tray	42, 48
Adding and removing items	48
Adding folders	49
FBI Internet Crime Complaint Center	177
Finding items	58-59
Fingerprint sensor	17
Fit app	116
Folders	
Adding to the Favorites Tray	49
Creating	49

G

Gallery app	155-156
Games	117
Gboard.	See also Keyboard
Adding text	93
Clipboard	91
GIF images	90
Numbers bar	86
One-handed	91
Stickers	90
Suggestion strip	90
Translate	91
Gmail	20, 102-105
Accessing	102
Accessing emails	104
Adding accounts	102-103
Adding attachments	105
Creating email	105
Formatting text	105
Setting up	102-103
Using	104-105
Google	10, 20, 58
Search options	58-61
Google Account	
About	20
From the Settings app	21
Obtaining	22
Payment	20
Google apps	110-111
Google Assistant	60-63
Google Discover	
Accessing	65
Discover	65
Google Docs	146-149
Google Drive	143-145
Google Lens	170
Google Maps	111
Google Pixel	10, 12
Google productivity apps	142
Google Search	60-61
When traveling	61
Google Search box	42, 58
Google Sheets	150-151

Google Slides   152
Google TV   20, 135-136
    For you   135
    Movies   136
    Shop   136
    TV shows   136

H

Hands-free   106
Hash key   79
Headphone jack   17
Health and fitness   116
Hey Google   62-64
Home button   45
Home screen   42
    Customizing app icons   53
    Favorites Tray   42
    Google Search box   42
    Main area   42
    Moving between   43
    Notifications bar   42
    Viewing   42
HTC   13
Huawei   13

I

IC3. *See* FBI Internet Crime Complaint Center
Instagram   115

K

Keyboard
    About   86-87
    Accented letters   92
    Auto-capitalization   89
    Auto-correction   89
    Back-delete   87, 93

Double-space period   89
Dual functions   92
Go button   87
Next-word suggestions   89, 93
Number pad   87
One-handed   91
Predictive text   88
Preferences   88
Send button   87
Settings   88-89
Shortcuts   92
Show suggestion strip   89, 93
Spacebar shortcut   92
Suggest Contacts   89
Symbols   87
Viewing   86
Keyboards   84
    Selecting   85
Kindle   139

L

Lenovo   13
Linux   8
Locating your phone   186
Locking
    Face   56
    Fingerprint   56
    Password   57
    Pattern   57
    PIN   57
    Swipe   56
    Your phone   56-57
Lock screen
    With Media Player   134
Losing your phone   176

M

macOS   8
Making a call   76-77
Malware   177

Managing apps   26
Maps   112-113
    Getting directions   113
    Viewing locations   112
Media Player   134
Memos   114
Messages app   96
Messaging.   See Texting
Messaging apps   72
Microphone
    Accessing   106
microSD cards   17
Micro USB port   17
Motorola   13
Music on Android   130-133

N

Navigation   43-45
News app   20
Nokia   13
Notes   114
Notifications   54-55
    Clearing   54
Notifications panel   42, 54
Notifications bar   54

O

Online protection   177
On/Off button   16
    For sleeping a phone   16
Organizing apps   49
Overlays   11

P

Parental controls   184-185
Payment

Through a Google Account   20
Phone
    Making a call   76-77
    Receiving a call   78-79
    Recents   70
Photos
    Adding   156-157
    Adding albums   161
    Cropping   163
    Editing   162-163
    From email   157
    Obtaining   156
    Sharing   164
    Transferring   157
    Viewing   158-159
Photos app   154-161
Pinterest   115
Play Books   20, 138
Play Store   20, 26, 46
    Categories   121
    Downloading apps   122-123
    Finding apps   120-121
    Navigating around   118-119
Podcasts   134
Power off   16

Q

Quick contact messaging   97
Quick Settings   40
QWERTY keyboard   87

R

Receiving calls   78-80
Recent Items button   45
Rejecting calls   78
Restart   16
Restricting access for children   176
Ringtones   81-82
    Downloading   82
Routers for Wi-Fi access   19

S

Samsung 12
Screen lock 56-57
Screen time 183
Searching 58-64
   Voice search 59-60
Security and privacy 178-179
Security issues 176
Selfies 17, 154
Settings
   About 39
   Accessibility 36-37
   Accessing 28
   Battery 34
   Connected devices 29
   Digital Wellbeing & parental controls 36
   Display 31
   Google 38
   Help 39
   Location 32
   Network & internet 29
   Notifications 34
   Passwords & accounts 33
   Safety & emergency 33
   Security & privacy 32
   Sound & vibration 30
   Storage 35
   System 39
   Wallpaper & style 31
Setting up 19
   Date and time 19
   Google Account 19
   Google services 19
   Language 19
   Method of screen lock 19
   Screen layout 19
   Wi-Fi 19
Sheets. See Google Sheets
SIM card 18
   eSIM 18
Sleep mode 16
Slides. See Google Slides
Snapchat 115

Social media 115
Sony 13
Swipe
   To unlock 56
Swiping
   On a web page 167

T

Text
   Adding 93
   Copy and paste 94
   Selecting 94
Texting 96-101
   Contacts 96-97
   Deleting conversation threads 96
   Emojis 98-99
   Large attachments 100
Touchscreen
   Pressing 25
   Protecting from moisture 24
   Swiping 25
   Tapping 25
   Using 24-25
TouchWiz interface 12
Turning off 16, 19
Turning on 16, 19
Twitter. See X

U

Uninstalling apps 124-125
Unlocking your phone 56-57
USB port
   For attaching to a computer 17
   For charging 17

V

Video calls	17
Videos	
Personal	
Adding	156
Virtual Contact File (VCF) file format	75
Viruses	176
Voice note	101
Voice typing	90
Volume button	16

W

Waking up from sleep	16
Wallpaper	52-53
Wallpaper apps	
Downloading	52
Web browsers	
Android	166
Web pages	
Navigating around	167
Websites	
Bookmarking pages	168-169
Browser settings	173-174
Images	170
Incognito browsing	172
Links	170
Mobile versions	166
Opening pages	167
Private browsing	172
Tabs	171
WhatsApp	72
Widgets	
Adding	50
Wi-Fi hotspots	29

X

X	115, 164

Y

YouTube	115
YT Music	
Accessing music	130
Explore	131
Home	130
Library	132
Upgrade	132

Z

Zooming in and out	
On web pages	167